THE WATER GARDENING
IDEA BOOK

HARDY NYMPHAEAS AND NELUMBIUMS

THE WATER GARDENING
IDEA BOOK

HOW TO BUILD, PLANT, AND MAINTAIN PONDS, FOUNTAINS, AND BASINS

PETER BISSET

Skyhorse Publishing

Skyhorse Publishing books may be purchased in bulk at special discounts for sales promotion, corporate gifts, fund-raising, or educational purposes. Special editions can also be created to specifications. For details, contact the Special Sales Department, Skyhorse Publishing, 307 West 36th Street, 11th Floor, New York, NY 10018 or info@skyhorsepublishing.com.

Skyhorse® and Skyhorse Publishing® are registered trademarks of Skyhorse Publishing, Inc.®, a Delaware corporation.

Visit our website at www.skyhorsepublishing.com.

10 9 8 7 6 5 4 3 2 1

Library of Congress Cataloging-in-Publication Data is available on file.

Cover design by Laura Shaw

Print ISBN: 978-1-62914-718-5
Ebook ISBN: 978-1-63220-181-2

Printed in China

AN AMATEUR'S WATER GARDEN

Contents

༷

Images

Preface

T HERE is no more fascinating pursuit connected with horticulture, none that gives greater pleasure and enjoyment to the owner, than the cultivation of a water garden. This is brought about from various reasons, chief among which is the important part played by water in all well-ordered landscape effects; secondly, the wealth and diversity of color, the great range of beauty, the interesting historical associations of many of the water plants employed, and their unique manner of flowering—for some varieties there are that unfold their untold loveliness when kissed by the first rays of the morning sun; others, again, like fairy craft, anchored in a miniature moonlit sea, disclose their gorgeousness and glory to the Queen of Night, and hold sweet communion with the silent stars. Then, too, there is the attractiveness which the plants necessary to the embellishment of the environments of a water garden present.

While the charm of running streams, lakes, and ponds in the landscape has ever been patent to all Nature lovers, it is only of late years that the intrinsic worth of the water garden proper and its lovely denizens, both vegetable and finny, as part of the adornment of public parks and home grounds, has become fully appreciated.

A little over three-fourths of a century ago the only plant of importance found in greater or less expanses of water, in most landscape designs, was the Richardia alba, popularly known as the Calla or Lily of the Nile, immense specimens of which are recorded. The beautiful native pondlilies, floating peacefully, silently, on the surface of pond or pool, their gorgeous blooms sparkling in the summer sun, had always been admired; collections of waterlilies had been gotten together by botanical institutions, but as yet their decorative value in garden work had not been fully realized.

We read that in England, in 1849, when the aquatic greenhouse was built at Chatsworth for the sole purpose of growing Victoria regia, Nymphaeas, and other water plants, it was regarded as a new departure in ornamental gardening. It was nearly thirty years later when the capabilities of waterlilies in garden work began to receive deserved attention in the United States, the seeming neglect of or indifference to them here being accounted for by the fact that the varieties then available were not of such color and character to appeal to the general public, being mostly tender kinds, needing special care and facilities possessed by but few growers. There was, of course, a fair number of varieties of the hardy white Nymphaeas, but it was not until the discovery of the pink sport of Nymphaea odorata on Cape Cod, and the introduction of Nymphaea alba rosea from Lake Fayer, Sweden, a few years afterward, that interest in these plants in America was quickened.

Perhaps the greatest impetus given to water gardening, both at home and abroad, resulted about the year 1887, when M. Marliac, a French specialist, introduced his magnificent hardy varieties, many of them still unsurpassed in shades of yellow, pink and red.

Since that time the enthusiasm in water gardening everywhere has kept on increasing. Hybridizers have been bringing forth new and improved varieties, both hardy and tender, of resplendent colors and graceful forms, and today there is hardly a garden of any pretensions without its waterlily pool or basin, quietly nestling amid its appropriate surroundings. Our park superintendents now fully recognize the attraction which the waterlily pond possesses for the general public, and are catering to this admirable popular taste by the installation of water gardens in these breathing spots of the people.

But it is not alone to the gardens of the wealthy, nor to the public parks, that the cultivation of waterlilies is confined. These plants are grown and admired by hundreds throughout the land to whom the art of gardening in its every phase forcibly appeals—a taste that is ever increasing with the growth of our population and which, above all others, reflects the refined character of our people. And it is a branch of gardening that comes well within the limits of the purse of the masses, the necessary first outlay for the full enjoyment of waterlily cultivation being practically nominal.

The volume now offered contains a record of the author's practical experience with this class of charming plants, extending over a period of over thirty years. It is a heart to heart talk, devoid of literary pretension, with those of kindred tastes to my own, and it is intended to form a working *vade mecum* which may lead to a better knowledge and a more complete understanding of everything connected with the cultivation of a race of garden subjects which, for beauty and grace, comprehensiveness of colors, and historical associations, to me, stands unrivaled in all Flora's realm.

The preparation of the illustrations contained in this volume, the great majority of which have been made by the author direct from the material obtainable in the water garden under his personal supervision, has been a labor of love for some years, and it is his trust that they will add to the interest of the book and prove an incitement to its readers.

For the preparation of the manuscript for the printer I am indebted to *The Florists Exchange* of New York.

I also desire to acknowledge the many valuable suggestions made and helpful aid otherwise rendered by A. T. De La Mare, president of the publishing firm, distributors of the work.

My earnest desire is that my interested readers, who follow the advice herein contained, will reap the great pleasure in this healthful branch of gardening practice that has been mine these many years.

PETER BISSET
Washington, D. C., November 1, 1924

Chapter I

FOREWORD

HISTORY records that from the earliest times it has been customary for mankind to recognize in certain plants and flowers some peculiar form of intrinsic beauty or economic value sufficient to induce the selection of these subjects from among their fellows as worthy of the highest adoration and honor. Such a distinction has been accorded waterlilies, dating back to the remotest ages. Students of botanical lore tell us that the Nymphaea lotus and N. coerulea, probably among the first plants to be thus singled out, were held sacred by the ancient Egyptians, the sculptured floral representations found among the ruins of temples in Egypt testifying to the veneration paid to these plants by the dwellers in the land of the Pharoahs. And Nelumbium speciosum was also worshiped, and deemed sacred by the natives of India, Tibet, China, and Japan, being to a greater or lesser extent still employed in religious invocations and ceremonies in these countires. One of the most exhaustive works dealing with a discussion of the Lotus is that excellent volume entitled, "The Grammar of the Lotus," by Professor Wm. H. Goodyear, M. A., curator of the Department of Fine Arts in the Brooklyn (N. Y.) Institute of Arts and Sciences. In that work Professor Goodyear points out that it is Nymphaea lotus or N. coerulea, the former the white, the latter the blue Lotus, and both native Egyptian plants, which are figured in the ornamental patterns of the monuments. "The 'Rose Lotus' Nelumbium speciosum," adds Professor Goodyear, "may possibly be realistically represented in ancient Egyptian paintings, just as the palm and many other plants appear, but such cases must be extremely rare, as none can be found in the great folio publications of Egyptian antiquities, or in the typical ornaments exhibited by Egyptian museums. As far as the typical ornaments or typical patterns are concerned, the 'Rose Lotus' is not to be found." It is now generally understood that this plant was introduced into Egypt from India, its native habitat.

Beauty of flower alone, however, was not the only quality possessed by the Nelumbium, compelling the admiration and veneration of the ancients, for the plant had as well utilitarian properties that appealed to them and rendered it of considerable economic value. The root stocks and seeds were prepared and eaten as food by the inhabitants of China, India, and Australia. In Cary's translation of Herodotus, speaking of the Egyptians, it is recorded as follows: "But to obtain food more easily, they have the following inventions: when the river is full, and has made the plains like a sea, great numbers of lilies, which the Egyptians call Lotus, spring up in the water; these they gather and dry in the sun; then having pounded the middle of the Lotus, which resembles a poppy, they make bread of it and bake it. The root also of this Lotus is fit for food, and is tolerably sweet, and is round and of the size of an apple. There are also other lilies resembling roses, that grow in the river, the fruit of which is contained in a separate pod that springs up from the root, in form very like a wasp's nest; in this there are many berries fit to be eaten, of the size of an olive stone, and they are eaten both fresh and dried." It is believed that from this statement of Herodotus the popular error has arisen that the Lotus was a native Egyptian plant, and, although he made no reference to the subject of Egyptian ornament, that Nelumbium speciosum was the typical sacred plant of Egypt. Nelumbium speciosum has also a medicinal value which lies in the viscid juice of the leaf stalks.

Though one species of Nelumbium—luteum, the charming yellow flowered Lotus—is indigenous to North America, it was not until some time in the seventies that Nelumbium speciosum (Nelumbo nucifera) reached this country from Japan through the instrumentality of the late Thomas Hogg, an Oriental traveler, who introduced many of our best known plants in cultivation from that wonderful country. Mr. Hogg sent roots of the Nelumbium speciosum to the late Isaac Buchanan, a florist, who planted them in a running stream on his grounds in Astoria, Long Island, but, unfortunately, they perished. At a subsequent date, Samuel Henshaw, a well known landscape gardener, narrates having received some roots from the same source, which he planted in an artificial pond in a garden on Staten Island, New York, where they grew and flourished. Mr. Henshaw's success with this and other aquatics led him to introduce water gardens into various landscape designs carried out by him, he having first become acquainted with the merits of the waterlilies at Chatsworth, England.

The cultivation of the Nelumbium as a commercial plant in the United States was first engaged in by the late E. D. Sturtevant, then of Borden town, N. J., who, about the same time as Mr. Henshaw received his tubers from Japan, secured a number from Kew Gardens, England. These were planted in a sheltered mill pond in shallow water where their hardiness was fully demonstrated, stock obtained from them being distributed to all parts of the United States.

No less interesting and beautiful are the various forms of Nymphaea, as well as the gigantic Victorias, historical data regarding the latter of which will be found in another chapter. Our native waterlily, Nymphaea odorata, was probably the first foreign Nymphaea to reach England, having, it is said, been introduced into that country about 1786, although the English species, Nymphaea alba, had been recognized long anterior to that date. In addition to their exquisite flowers some of the Nymphaeas possess economic properties. The root stocks of Nymphaea alba contain gallic acid, and on that account are said to be useful for dyeing purposes.

Waterlilies are found in a wild state in nearly all of the countries of the world. From South America we get the well known Victoria regia; from Mexico, Nymphaea mexicana and Nymphaea gracilis; from our own country come the charming Nymphaea odorata, Nymphaea tuberosa, Nymphaea flava, Nymphaea elegans, and the beautiful Nelumbium luteum already mentioned. From Europe we get the chaste white waterlily, Nymphaea alba; the red colored one, Nymphaea alba rosea, which is a native of Sweden; also Nymphaea Candida from Bohemia. From far off Australia comes one of the finest of the blue waterlilies, Nymphaea gigantea. From China we get that little gem, Nymphaea tetragona or pygmaea; from India the deep, red colored, night flowering Nymphaea rubra, likewise the first cousin of the Victoria regia, Euryale ferox; from Egypt the Nymphaea lotus, and from Africa the deep royal purple Nymphaea zanzibariensis, while from Japan the many beautiful and stately forms of the Nelumbium are obtained.

The colors of the flowers range from the purest white through soft delicate shades of pink to the deepest reds; from the deepest purple through the lighter shades of blue to the palest blue imaginable, and from pale yellow through the deeper shades to salmon.

Nearly all of the flowers have a delicious fragrance, ranging from the delicate tea odor of Nymphaea tetragona through the stronger scented Nymphaea odorata to the almost overpowering vanilla-scented Victoria regia.

There is also a great difference in the hours of expanding their blooms. Many of the waterlilies open their flowers soon after daybreak, others later in the morning, remaining open for the greater part of the day; while the evening is ushered in by the opening of the night flowering Nymphaea lotus, Nymphaea rubra and their host of varieties, these remaining open throughout the night and well on to noon of the following day; the enchanting Victoria regia also throws open its cream colored flowers as the day darkens into night.

> "Misty moonlight, faintly falling
> O'er the lake at eventide,
> Shows a thousand gleaming lilies
> On the rippling waters wide.
>
> "White as snow, the circling petals
> Cluster round each golden star,
> Rising, falling, with the waters,
> Moving, yet at rest they are.
>
> "Winds may blow, and skies may darken,
> Rain may pour, and waves may swell;
> Deep beneath the changeful eddies
> Lily roots are fastened well."

Waterlilies differ from each other not only in the color of their blooms and their time of opening, but also in the length of their flower stems. Many of the blossoms float on the surface of the water; others have stems that carry the flowers from three to fifteen inches above the surface, the blooms ranging in size from those of the little Nymphaea pygmaea of two inches to that of the wonderful Nymphaea dentata of fifteen inches in diameter.

The plants also differ in the characteristics and color of their foliage; many have floating leaves, others have the center leaves raised above the water, especially those of Nymphaea tuberosa ancestry. Some of the leaves are green, others reddish bronze, while many are beautifully mottled with chocolate spots on a green ground.

The great variation in the form of flower, in the colors, and in the growth of the plants, coming as they do from many countries, lend to the occupants of the water garden a charm and a fascination that no other style of garden possesses.

Chapter II

PONDS AND BASINS

Concerning the Importance of a Carefully Selected Site

I N selecting the location of a pond, or pool, in which to grow waterlilies, the ground should be gone over carefully, and a site chosen where a supply of water, either from a natural stream or from an artificial source, will be provided. The location should, if possible, be sheltered by buildings, by a planting of trees and shrubs far enough away from the edge of the pond that they will not overshadow the water, or by a high bank on the northwest, northeast, and north, but open toward the south, southwest, and southeast. This will insure the full benefit of the sun's rays in warming the water, and, at the same time, afford protection from high winds that soon would ruin the tropical growth of the tender waterlilies and the subtropical plants in the surrounding borders. If the pond is intended for the growth of hardy kinds only, it will not be necessary to protect it, as these will thrive in a much lower temperature than the tender ones, and the leaf surface of the hardy sorts is so small that they are never seriously damaged by the wind.

Making Artificial Ponds

Having decided upon the location of the pond, stakes should be driven into the ground, a few feet apart, outlining the edge. In making a pond for the cultivation of waterlilies for pleasure, it is well not to have it so wide that one cannot enjoy the flowers at close range. The greatest width should not exceed 75 feet. The flowers never rise above the water more than fifteen inches, except in the case of the Nelumbiums, which grow to a height of from two to eight feet out of the water. But, with waterlilies proper, one has to get near them to enjoy the full beauty and exquisite coloring of the flowers.

If it is desired to have a greater expanse of water than one 75 feet in width, an island, located near the center of the pond and connected with the mainland by a rustic footbridge, should be formed. This island, which should be irregular in outline, and of varying width and height, will afford an opportunity to utilize many rare and beautiful plants suitable for the margins, also flowering shrubs and trees, which, by a judicious selection and careful planting so that they will not shade the pond, will add materially to the charm of the whole when finished. The outline of the island could be marked, at intervals, by heavy boulders, or rocks, so placed as to create a natural effect.

The location and size of the pond decided upon, and the outline marked by the stakes, a level should be taken from a point determined either by a natural feature, the supply of water, or the surface of the ground. For best effect the pond should be slightly below the surrounding level, as this will permit of plants being grown right up to the water's edge, and present a more natural appearance than if the edge of the pond or pool were elevated above the ground. If the pond is to be a large one and one is not skilled in the use of the spirit level, or the surveyor's instrument, it will be advisable to get a surveyor to run the levels, so that they shall be exact.

After securing the levels, the soil is excavated and thrown up on the banks, or carted away to fill depressions, or low ground, in the neighborhood of the pond. As the pond will generally be located in the lowest part of the grounds, existing depressions filled in with this surplus soil and elevated to the same level will add much to the beauty of the whole. The sides of the pond should slope at an angle of from 40 to 45 degrees if to be puddled with clay.

The pond should be excavated to a depth of two feet six inches. This will allow of four inches of clay on the bottom, eight inches of soil, and one foot six inches of water. If the method of growing the plants in boxes or tubs is to be practiced, the boxes would take the place of the soil, and should be about twelve inches in depth.

If the soil is of a sandy or gravelly nature, through which the water will drain off, some means must then be employed to make the pond watertight, so as to avoid this waste, and provide against the reduction of the temperature of the water through having to supply more to take the place of that lost. Water from springs, or from an open stream, is generally from 15 to 20 degrees colder than that already in the pond which has been warmed by the sun's rays, and will lower the temperature of the water in the pond considerably if the loss by seepage is very great. The common method, and the least expensive in first cost, is to puddle the bottom and sides of the pond with clay. This material can be obtained in nearly all localities if one digs deep enough to secure it. The clay is taken in slices of about four inches in thickness, of uniform size, and is placed on the sides and bottom of the pond in the same manner that sod is laid down to secure a lawn. Then the whole is rammed hard and smooth with a heavy rammer, care being taken that all joints are closed and no apertures left through which the water can escape. If the clay is too hard to be easily beaten into place it can be made plastic by sprinkling water over it, allowing it to soften a little, when it can be rammed into place.

If a good grade of clay, that will cut into slices, is not available, as stiff a clay as can be procured should be taken, chopped into small pieces, mixed with water, turned and chopped several times until all is of the consistency of stiff putty or mortar; this can then be spread over the bottom and sides, in layers until of the thickness of four inches or more; and after the whole has dried somewhat it can be tamped in place. While this puddling method is the most economical as regards first cost, it really is the most expensive in the end, as the clay is always in more or less danger of being displaced by the attendant walking around the pond while caring for the plants. The clay is also very easily penetrated by that great pest of all such ponds, the crawfish.

An Excellent Material for Artificial Pond Making

The very best material that can be used for the formation of all ponds, tanks, and pools is, without doubt, hydraulic cement. An inexpensive and easily made artificial stone can be had that will stand the test of all climates, proof against all boring pests, and at the same time will not cost much more than the clay method described. If cement for the walls and bottom is to be used, this decision should be reached before any of the soil is excavated. After the pond has been outlined, another row of stakes should be inserted from six to twelve inches away from the first, forming a double row of stakes. The soil between these rows of stakes should be excavated to the required depth of the pond by use of a drain spade, care being taken not to damage the sides of the ditch in digging, as this excavation will act as a mold for the wall. If, by misadventure, the sides should be damaged, repair the same by inserting rough boards, so as to have the wall of uniform width. The width of the wall will depend on the degree of frost pressure that will be exerted upon it during the winter. Six inches in width will be ample where the winters are mild; but for the neighborhood of Washington, D. C, and farther north, the width must be from nine to twelve inches. It is advisable to have the walls wider at the bottom than at the top. They should slope toward the top on both sides; this will allow the soil, in freezing, to lift upward, and so reduce the pressure on the walls.

After the soil has been excavated from this space, the level of the wall should be determined, and stakes driven in as guides, so that the top of the wall when finished shall be six inches below the level of the surface ground. This will allow of grass, or other plants, to be grown on the top of the wall, thus hiding it and presenting a natural view in harmony with the environments; or the wall may be carried up to form a coping. The space excavated should be filled in with concrete, composed of one part Portland cement, three parts sand, four parts gravel, and three parts broken stone. First mix the sand and cement by turning until thoroughly incorporated, then mix the gravel and broken stone with the cement and sand. The whole should be turned several times until the different ingredients are thoroughly intermixed, when water should be added, and the mass turned until it is of the nature of a sticky paste; add the water sparingly, or some of the cement will be washed away.

When the concrete is ready, it can be conveyed in wheelbarrows to the excavation, poured in, and rammed into position. The stones used should not be larger than two inches in diameter, and the gravel from one and a quarter inches down to the size of a pea, the aim being to have sufficient of the small gravel to fill all the interstices between the stones, and the sand and cement to fill in between the small gravel, making the whole wall one solid stone. Care should be taken to secure a good solid foundation or the walls will be apt to crack through settling. If the ground is soft, large stones should be rammed in to give sufficient foundation on which to build the walls.

Excavating

After the wall has dried out sufficiently, the work of excavating the pond proper can be proceeded with. Remove all the soil to the level of the bottom of the wall, then place a large pipe at the bottom and near the end where the overflow will'be, to act as a draw-off pipe for the emptying of the pond.

A fair-sized hole should be made below the level of this pipe, somewhere in the pond, to provide a pool for the fish when the water is drawn off. The bottom of the pond should be covered with six inches of concrete, mixed the same as that for the walls, and well rammed. After the whole is completed in the rough and all soil adhering to the sides removed, a one-inch coating of cement and sand should be put on the walls and bottom, composed of one part Portland cement to three parts finely screened sand, mixed with water, and applied with a smoothing trowel, to give a perfectly smooth surface.

VICTORIA REGIA IN LINCOLN PARK, CHICAGO, ILL.

Natural Ponds

So far we have only treated of artificial ponds, or pools, which require excavation. In many places there are natural ponds which, at little expense, can be made very beautiful and a joy to their owners. First consider the source of the water supply: is it subject from any cause to a wash that would render it at times unsightly by the quantity of muddy water carried into it by heavy rains? Or is there a stream passing through the pond from, springs which, being colder, will lower the temperature of the water it contains? All streams should be diverted so that they cannot enter the pond unless desired by the owner or caretaker. This can be easily done by an open ditch, dug so as to skirt the pond, and at some distance from it. The banks can be adorned with a choice collection of plants that will thrive in such a place. Or the stream, if not too large, can be led through a terra cotta pipe to a point below the pond where it can then proceed on its natural course. The water supply can be taken from the stream at a point where the source is above the level of the pond, and the water let in through a terra cotta pipe, or by an open ditch which can be made very beautiful by planting the sides of it with moisture-loving plants, a list of which will be found enumerated in another chapter. Some means should be provided for closing the pipe automatically, so that the flow of water can be cut off in time of storm, or at the will of the owner. The author has worked out a very satisfactory arrangement for this purpose. The supply pipe is fitted with a "sewer pipe gate," which is shown in detail in the sketch "Inlet for Water to Pond." The water from the stream passes through a screen of quarter-inch galvanized wire mesh, flowing around the sides of the gate into the inlet pipe. The ball float will rise and fall with the depth of water in the stream, adjusting itself automatically. The volume of water to be admitted into the pond is controlled by bending the rod of the ball float. When the stream is swollen by a storm and an inflow of muddy water, the ball float rises, completely closing the inlet so that no water passes through the pipe until the stream has regained its normal level. When it is desired to admit the full capacity of the pipe, the ball can be unscrewed, allowing the gate to open wide. This gate can be purchased from any dealer in plumbers' supplies, and any intelligent machinist or plumber can fit up the arrangement as described.

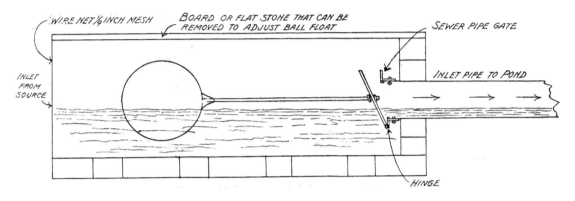

INLET FOR WATER TO POND
Showing a satisfactory device by which storm water is excluded from the water garden

If no stream is available the water can be taken from a well, or from the city supply where such exists. Wherever it can be carried out the supply should flow into the pond naturally; that is to say, without being forced in by means of a pump. If, however, this is not practicable, a hydraulic ram is an inexpensive and efficient means to elevate the water to the desired height. A ram of the smallest size requires a flow of from two to three gallons of water per minute to work it, and a fall or head of three feet; with this head the ram will pump from ten to fifteen gallons of water per hour, raising the water to a height from fifteen to twenty feet above the level of the ram. For every additional head of a foot the ram will raise the water from five to ten feet higher. Rams can be purchased of sufficient capacity to deliver up to four gallons of water per minute.

Another very satisfactory means to lift the water to a higher level is to use a water wheel on the axle of which is placed an eccentric; to this is attached the piston of the pump. This is a very economical arrangement to lift water, the wheel being in perfect control by means of a valve placed on the feed pipe that supplies the water to drive the wheel. One point in which it is superior to the ram is that the water required to drive the wheel is not wasted, as the suction pipe from the pump can be placed in the rear of the wheel, the water, after passing over the wheel, can be pumped up. This will be of great importance where the water supply is limited. The wheel is operated with but small attention, as there is little about it to get out of order, it merely requires that the oil cups on the bearings be kept supplied with oil, and new suction cups placed in the pump as needed.

If it is not practicable to use either of these methods a windmill or gasoline engine can be employed to lift the water.

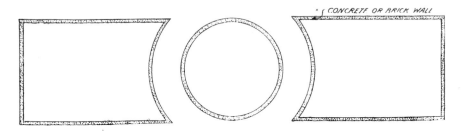

A TERRACE WATER GARDEN
A suggestion for a water garden on the top of a terrace. The circular pool to
be filled with Nelumbiums, the side pools with hardy or tender waterlilies

It is not necessary, nor desirable, that a stream of water should be continually passing into the pond if tender lilies are growing in it. All that is required is that the water lost through evaporation or leakage be replaced by a fresh supply. Many are afraid of malaria and mosquitoes proceeding from a pond unless a continuous stream of water is passing through it; this fear is groundless. If a pond is properly stocked with plant growth, and with a sufficient number of fish of the proper kinds, there will be no malaria or stagnation. And as for the mosquitoes, if there are fish enough in the pond they will take care of all the larvae so that not one of these will ever reach the adult stage.

For small tanks, or pools, located on the lawn near the dwelling house, and made of concrete or masonry, walls and bottom, a water supply that will be found adequate for all purposes in the Northeastern States, or where the rainfall is sufficient, can be provided by the watershed from the roof of the dwelling, led through a pipe into the pool. This supply will be found ample to restore all loss by evaporation, and will keep the water in good condition for the growth of aquatic plants.

It is always desirable to have a pipe of sufficient capacity laid from the bottom of the pond, or tank, to the waste way or stream that carries off the waste or overflow of water, it being necessary to empty the pond or tank at least twice a year for the proper preparation of soil and the planting, and again in the fall for the removal of the roots of the tender lilies. This pipe should be of large size so that the work of emptying can be done quickly. A straightway or gate valve fitted to this pipe, and located on the bank just outside the pond will be found very helpful and a great convenience when it becomes necessary to empty the water.

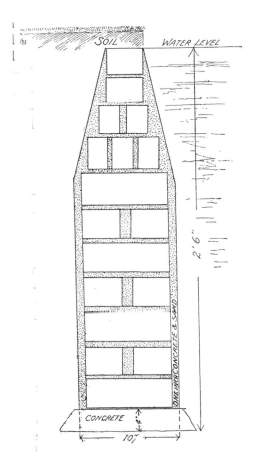

Plan for a brick wall, on a foundation of concrete faced with one inch of sand and cement mortar

Another method of securing a natural pond, and one often pursued, where a stream of water runs through the place, is to form a dam across the stream the soil being excavated gives the pond the desired shape and used to make the dam or to bring the surrounding ground up to a level. This style of pond, however, is rarely satisfactory and is not to be recommended. The dam is always a weak point, and being "made earth" the water can easily percolate through it and cause a leak. The stream will also have to be diverted so as to prevent it flooding the pond, an operation which will about equalize the cost of excavating the entire pond.

BASINS FOR THE AMATEUR

These can be made of concrete as already described or built of brick as desired. The depth will be the same as that recommended for the larger ponds, namely, two feet six inches. If it is decided to construct the walls of brick, they should be built as shown in the illustration and the two sides of the walls covered with a coating of cement and sand using sand that has passed through a fine screen. The proportions of this facing mortar should be one part of best Portland cement to three parts of sand. Care should be taken in all cement work not to allow a too rapid drying of the cement; the slower cement mortar hardens or sets, the stronger the material will be.

To make the bottom of the pool watertight, the bricks can be laid flat with from one-half to one-inch apertures between them, these are filled in with the same mortar as recommended for facing the side walls. The top of the walls should have a coating of the same mortar or be capped with a stone coping.

The basin, or pool, can be located on the lawn, near the dwelling, as then the flowers can be seen at any hour of the day. The time to see the waterlily pool at its best is about 10 a.m. At that time the night blooming lilies have not yet closed and the day flowering tender and hardy ones will be open so that the face of the water will be covered with flowers. Morning, generally, is a very busy time and the sun during our summer months is nearly always hot. Therefore, one is rarely inclined to visit the water garden about that time, especially if it be located at a distance from the house. Hence the advantage of having the basin as near to the dwelling as possible.

AN OLD MILL LEAD ON AN AMATEUR'S
PLACE, BEFORE PLANTING

Photograph by Mrs. Helen Ripley Eustis, North
Tisbury, Mass.

THE SAME MILL LEAD THE FOLLOWING JUNE
showing what a beautiful spot can be evolved from an
unsightly object, by means of suitable plants and a taste-
ful arrangement. German and Japanese Iris with ferns on
the left side; Siberian Iris on the right

Photograph by Mrs. Helen Ripley Eustis,
North Tisbury, Mass.

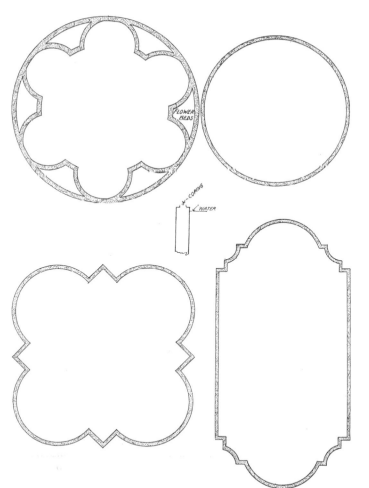

SUGGESTIVE DESIGNS FOR SMALL
WATER GARDENS ON THE LAWN
A basin of circular shape with a coping of stone
or cement will look well on any lawn of large
extent. If the lawn is of small size, with straight
walks in proximity to the basin, one of oblong
shape will be more desirable

The shape of the basin will depend on the architecture of the house and the design of the grounds. If formal or natural plantings have been adopted, the lily basin should conform as near as possible to its surroundings, that the whole, when completed, may be in perfect harmony. A basin of circular shape, with a coping of stone or cement, will look well on any lawn of large extent. This may be embellished by the addition of a fountain rising from the center, which may be put in operation for a short time at rare intervals, especially after a warm day when the lilies will be benefited by a shower. But this fountain should never be allowed to play on the water lilies for any length of time, as the colder water entering the basin will reduce the temperature to a point lower than it should be for best results. If the lawn is of small size, with straight walks in proximity to the basin, one of oblong shape will be more desirable, as its straight lines will harmonize better with the walks than a basin of circular form.

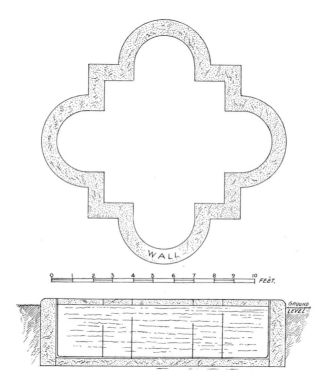

SUGGESTION FOR A WATERLILY BASIN ON A LAWN,
SHOWING A SECTION OF THE SAME

If the cost of building a cement basin exceeds the amount one desires to expend, very good results can be obtained by purchasing a large hogshead, sawing it in two and sinking the tubs thus formed into the lawn so that the edges will be level with the grass. Waterlilies or Nelumbiums planted in these tubs will give many beautiful flowers. A series of such tubs can be arranged that will be very attractive. Place a large one, filled with Nelumbiums, in the center, and surround this larger one with a number of smaller tubs, filled with a selection of the hardy or tender day flowering lilies. If these tubs be coated with tar on the outside to preserve the wood and buried to their edge in the grass, they will look more natural. A selection of Japanese Iris, or any fern or other moisture-loving plant desired, can be planted between the tubs.

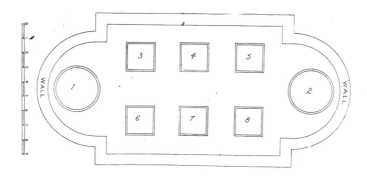

A SMALL WATERLILY BASIN FOR THE LAWN
It is suggested that No. 1 be planted with Nelumbium speciosum;
No. 2 with Nelumbium pekinense rubrum; No. 3 with Nymphaea
gladstoniana; No. 4 with Nymphaea zanzibariensis; No. 5 with
Nymphaea marliacea chromatella; No. 6 with Nymphaea marlia-
cea rosea; No. 7 with Nymphaea Mrs. C. W. Ward; No. 8 with
Nymphaea gloriosa
The circles and squares represent half barrels and boxes in which
to grow the plants

One need never be deterred from growing this beautiful class of plants for want of a basin; the lilies will do better in a basin without a doubt, but excellent results have been obtained by using half barrels, set on the surface of the ground, placing one plant in each receptacle.

Whatever style of basin is adopted, the requirements are practically the same—sufficient good, rich soil with at least six inches of water above it, and two goldfish in each half barrel to keep down mosquitoes. When goldfish are placed in the barrels it is well to have some other vessel plunged in the soil so as to afford the fish a hiding place from the cat, as pussy is generally fond of fish, and if the water in the basin or pool be shallow she can easily reach them.

A FOUNTAIN BASIN
Center filled with Myriophyllum proserpinacoides (Parrotfeather)

Chapter III

WINDBREAKS AND MARGINS

THE waterlily pond, or basin, should be fully protected from the cold and high windstorms generally prevalent from the north, northwest and sometimes from the northeast. If no buildings or nearby hillsides afford this protection, recourse must be had to a wall, a hedge, or a belt of evergreen or deciduous trees, so planted as to answer the purpose in view. The amount of space available will decide the method of protection. If the space be limited, there is nothing better than an evergreen hedge of Norway Spruce (Picea excelsa); this is a fine hardy evergreen, of dense habit of growth, well suited to form a windbreak. It grows quickly, reaching at maturity a height of from 60 to 100 feet, while in favorable localities it will attain a height of 150 feet. The branches are slender, in regular pseudo-whorls from the base up; the branches are gently decurved with the tips upturned, the higher branches spread horizontally, while the uppermost ones point upward. This fir can be cut back every year, as is an ordinary hedge of Privet; or it can be planted from three to twelve feet apart and allowed to grow naturally.

Another good evergreen for this purpose is Thuja occidentalis, the American Arborvitae. This is a fine hardy evergreen, and one of the best hedge plants for screens and windbreaks, especially if the ground space is limited. It is a tall, upright growing tree, with a spread of four to six feet, attaining a height of from 30 to 60 feet, with very dense foliage. This tree can also be sheared every year, as is done with a hedge plant, but the effect will be better if the trees are planted three feet apart and allowed to grow naturally.

Tsuga canadensis (Hemlock Spruce) is another beautiful evergreen well adapted for a hedge; it is indeed an ideal tree for a windbreak, either grown naturally or planted close and treated as a hedge plant. It is a very hardy tree, and where it gets enough sunlight it will be furnished with branches to the ground. The branches are slender and spreading; the lower ones deflex by their own weight; the foliage is of a dark green color above, and silvery gray underneath.

While only three kinds have been mentioned, any evergreen can be used that grows sufficiently close, and that will succeed in the locality where the planting is done.

If the grounds are extensive, and a broad belt of planting can be carried out, it is well to have a background of large deciduous trees, such as Oaks, Beeches, Maples, Lindens and Tulip Poplars; while in the foreground can be planted some of the more valuable evergreen trees, such as Pinus strobus, the American White Pine, which is one of the noblest of evergreens, growing from 80 to 100 feet in height. Its slender, threadlike leaves are from three to four inches in length, of bluish green color with silvery lines, giving the tree a silvery blue effect. The White Pine losing its lower branches as it gets older, it should be planted next to the deciduous trees.

Pinus excelsa, the Bhotan Pine, is a very handsome tree, with long, drooping slender leaves of grayish green color, from five to seven inches in length. The tree grows to a height of from 50 to 150 feet; it is a native of the Himalaya Mountains, and is well adapted for windbreaks, for, unlike Pinus strobus, when planted in a favorable location it retains its lower branches to the ground, making a tree not only valuable as a windbreak, but, with its long, slender leaves, giving the effect of a graceful weeping tree. It is also a beautiful specimen for the lawn.

Pinus cembra is another fine dense growing medium-sized tree, of from 50 to 70 feet in height, with silvery green foliage and branches down to the ground; it is one of the finest of the Pines for lawn planting.

Pinus austriaca, the Austrian Pine, is one of the hardiest of the Pine family, of dense growth in the young state, with very dark green, rigid leaves, three to five inches in length. This tree also loses its lower branches as it gets older; when full grown it will be without limbs for about one-half its height. It grows from 60 to 100 feet high, and with its very dark green, almost black foliage, is an excellent tree for the background as a setting for the more valuable ones.

In Abies nordmanniana we have one of the best of the Firs, a beautiful subject with dense, dark green foliage, and silvery white underneath. The branches are rigid, horizontal, or ascending. The tree grows from 75 to 150 feet in height.

Abies cephalonica is a strong, vigorous tree, reaching a height of from 50 to 60 feet, with wide spreading horizontal branches, and dark, lustrous, green leaves.

Abies concolor is a beautiful tree of close, dense growth; it has light, glaucous green leaves, giving the tree an attractive color of bluish white.

A WINDBREAK OF PINES AND SPRUCES FOR THE PROTECTION
OF THE WATER GARDEN

Picea pungens glauca kosteri (Koster's form of the Colorado Blue Spruce), is the bluest form of the Spruce family. The type comes from the mountains of Colorado, and has beautiful silvery blue colored leaves. It grows to a height of from 80 to 100 feet, has stout, rigid, horizontal branches, and a fine, dense habit of growth. It is a good ornamental lawn tree as well as being useful as a windbreak.

In front of the evergreens above mentioned, the smaller growing ones should also be planted, such as the golden Arborvitae, Thuja occidentalis lutea (T. George Peabody); this is a fine, low tree of pyramidal habit of growth; the young foliage of the current year's growth is bright yellow, the older foliage green variegated with yellow.

Thuja occidentalis vervaeneana is a smaller and denser tree than the type; the branchlets of the current year's growth are tinged with deep golden yellow, changing in winter to brownish orange.

Thuja occidentalis fastigiata (T. o. pyramidalis) is a fine evergreen of a tall, narrow, fastigiate form, and close green leaves.

Thuja occidentalis wareana is another tree of denser growth and deeper, brighter green foliage than the type; the branches are short, horizontal at first, then ascending.

Thuja occidentalis sibirica is a dense growing pyramidal evergreen, with deep green leaves, which retain their color well through the winter; is very hardy, and makes a fine lawn specimen, being also valuable as a hedge plant for windbreaks.

Libocedrus decurrens is another fine, dark, glossy, green leaved evergreen, of tall, columnar habit, growing from 100 to 150 feet in height; it makes a beautiful specimen.

Thuja plicata (gigantea) is another evergreen of fine, dense habit; it has dark green leaves and grows to a height of from 150 to 200 feet. This, unlike the common Arborvitae, stays green all winter, while the latter turns a deep brown at the approach of cold weather.

Chamaecyparis obtusa is a tall growing tree, eventually reaching a height of from 70 to 100 feet. It is of pyramidal growth in the young state, with branches to the ground; as it gets older the tree loses its lower branches and assumes a rounded top. This is a beautiful evergreen.

Chamaecyparis obtusa aurea is a fine variety similar to the type, with deep golden yellow foliage during the growing season.

Chamaecyparis pisifera is a smaller and more slender tree than C. obtusa; the foliage is dark green, with a decided yellow tinge during the growing season.

Chamaecyparis pisifera aurea is one of the best yellow colored evergreens, the whole growth of the current year being of a rich yellow which fades to the normal color the second year. This variety is quite distinct from C. plumosa aurea and is a better tree.

Chamaecyparis pisifera filifera is a fine, low growing tree, with deep green foliage; the young growth is threadlike and pendant, giving a graceful, weeping habit and forming a close growing, attractive tree.

Chamaecyparis pisifera filifera aurea is a beautiful variety with all of the current year's growth colored a light golden yellow.

Chamaecyparis pisifera plumosa is a tree with dense, dark green foliage and a conical habit of growth.

Chamaecyparis pisifera plumosa aurea is a variety of C. pisifera plumosa, the terminal growth of the current year being of a light golden yellow.

WATER'S EDGE PLANTING—HARDY HYBRID RHODODENDRONS
From left to right: R. album elegans, R. President Lincoln, R. roseum elegans

Chamaecyparis pisifera squarrosa veitchi is the best form of the squarrosa type. The foliage is of a beautiful silvery blue, similar to that of a fine form of the Colorado Blue Spruce. The leaves are very fine, arranged in spirals, giving the tree a beautiful graceful effect.

In the foreground of the trees named should be planted a choice assortment of flowering shrubs; or, if more desirable, a number of the dwarf evergreens, such as Picea excelsa pumila, a dwarf, compact Spruce of perfect, symmetrical habit.

Picea excelsa pumila compacta grows from five to six feet in height and has dark green, compact foliage.

Juniperus sabina is a spreading shrub or low tree of variable habit; it grows from four to ten feet in height.

Juniperus sabina prostrata is a low growing evergreen, lying flat on the ground; it has light, bluish green leaves.

Juniperus sabina tamariscifolia is a low spreading, vigorous variety, with bright green leaves.

Juniperus communis aurea (Douglas Golden Juniper) is a beautiful, low growing, yellow colored evergreen; the young growth is a brilliant yellow during the growing season.

Juniperus chinensis albo-variegata is a dwarf evergreen of dense columnar habit, many of the branchlets being cream white in color.

Juniperus chinensis aurea is a beautiful plant, with all of the young growth a golden yellow color.

Juniperus chinensis procumbens is a dwarf, low spreading evergreen.

Juniperus chinensis procumbens aurea is a variety of the preceding, having the young growth tinged with yellow.

In Juniperus chinensis procumbens aurea variegata many of the young branchlets are tinged with deep golden yellow.

Chamaecyparis obtusa pygmaea (Retinospora) is a very desirable, low growing evergreen, of deep color, rarely reaching more than two feet in height. It is of dense growth, spreading horizontally.

Chamaecyparis obtusa aurea is a small growing form, with deep golden yellow foliage.

Pinus montana (P. mughus) is a low growing, rigid Pine, of semi-prostrate habit. It has dark green foliage.

The foregoing forms a list of trees, all of which are well suited to protect the pond from wind, and at the same time will provide a beautiful and interesting border of trees.

Whatever trees are selected, they should be planted in an irregular belt if the width of the ground will allow of this being done. By so doing a more natural planting will be obtained, and an undulating margin that will present a much better appearance than if the trees are planted in straight rows.

All of the subjects mentioned above are suitable for windbreaks, but they will not succeed on low, wet, swampy soil; if the surroundings of the pond are of this character, the ground should be drained and filled to a higher level if this is possible. If this is not practicable, then a planting of such trees as succeed well in low, wet ground should be selected, such as Platanus acerifolia (the London Plane). This is a stately, wide spreading tree, of vigorous, quick growth and heavy foliage.

Liriodendron tulipifera (White Wood or Tuliptree) succeeds well in low, wet soil. It grows rapidly, forming a large, broad spreading tree, with fine, light, bluish green foliage. The tree bears in spring tulip-shaped flowers of a yellowish green color. It is best to transplant young trees of the Liriodendron in spring; if old trees are moved they rarely survive the operation, and seldom live if moved in the fall.

Courtesy H. P. Kelsey, Salem, Mass.
WATER'S EDGE PLANTING—RHODODENDRON MAXIMUM, THE GREAT-LEAVED LAUREL
A fine hardy evergreen flowering shrub

Nyssa sylvatica (Sourgum) is another native tree well adapted for low, wet situations. It is a tall tree of slender habit, growing from 40 to 60 feet in height, with small, obovate or oval, glossy, leathery leaves that turn a bright, beautiful, flaming scarlet in the fall.

Liquidambar styraciflua (Sweetgum) is a tree also of value for its beautiful colored leaves in fall, which range from the greens through yellow, purplish red to deep bronzy black, often all of these colors being present in the one leaf. It likes a low, wet, marshy place. The leaves are palmate, five-to seven-lobed, on leaf stalks six to seven inches long; the bark takes on a corky effect that is very interesting. The tree grows to a height of from 40 to 100 feet, according to the location. This is one of the best of the swamp trees.

Quercus bicolor (Swamp White Oak) is a native, growing to a height of from 60 to 70 feet. The head is narrow and rounded; the leaves are four to seven inches long, the trunk covered with light gray bark. It likes a low, wet position.

Quercus palustris (Pin Oak) is another native tree, growing from 60 to 120 feet in height. It is quick growing, and has beautiful, deeply cut foliage with a decided yellow color to the young, unfolding leaves, which take on brilliant fall hues. It is a fine tree for low, wet ground, and is also the easiest of all the Oaks to transplant.

Acer rubrum (Swamp or Red Maple) is a tree that will do well in any location; in the swamp or on the dry hillside it is perfectly at home. This tree has a beautiful, symmetrically rounded head when grown where it has room to develop. The flowers are bright red in spring; the leaves, in fall, turn bright yellow or scarlet, tinting the swamps all over the Eastern States with their beautiful colors.

Betula nigra is a fine tree for low ground, growing from 50 to 90 feet in height. It has reddish brown bark, silvery gray on the young branches.

Betula occidentalis reaches a height of from 30 to 40 feet and has slender branches and broad, ovate leaves; it grows well in wet soil.

Salix babylonica (Weeping Willow) is a beautiful weeping tree, very well adapted for growing in low, wet ground. It reaches a height of from 30 to 40 feet and has long, slender, drooping, olive green branches.

Salix babylonica aurea is a variety of Salix babylonica, with bright yellow bark that is very ornamental, especially in winter.

Salix vitellina aurea (Salix vitellina aurantiaca), (Golden Willow) is a very effective tree; in winter the branches and twigs are of a beautiful yellow color.

In the immediate foreground should be planted Magnolia glauca, the Swamp Magnolia or Sweet-bay. This is a fine shrub or small evergreen tree. The leaves are bluish green above, with a silvery white reverse. The flowers are very sweet-scented, of globular form, and cream colored when first opening. This Magnolia is quite at home in the swamps, but it also thrives in moist soil on higher ground.

Kalmia latifolia delights in a moist, peaty soil, and grows very well in swampy places if planted on low mounds. It is one of the most charming of the native flowering shrubs. The flowers, borne in large terminal clusters, are rose colored to white, with purple spots. It attains a height of from four to twelve feet.

Rhododendron maximum, the Great-leaved Laurel, is a native Rhododendron of extreme hardiness, growing from ten to twenty feet in height. The leaves are narrow and oblongs from four to ten inches in lengthy bright green above, grayish white underneath. The flowers are borne in large clusters, colored pale rose with greenish spots within.

KALMIA LATIFOLIA AT THE EDGE OF A POND
One of the most charming of the native flowering shrubs

Rhododendron maximum roseum is identical with the type, except in the flower, which is pink colored.

Rhododendron catawbiense is a native Rhododendron that never grows as tall as Rhododendron maximum, and is less desirable than it as a garden plant, except in high altitudes. It grows at a higher elevation than Rhododendron maximum, hence is not as well adapted to low ground as that plant. The flowers are lilac purple in color, the plant reaching a height of from six to fifteen feet. It is perfectly hardy in the New England States.

Rhododendron punctatum is a smaller growing plant, never reaching over six feet in height. The branches are slender and spreading. The flowers, which are colored pale rose with green spots, are borne in small clusters. This is a very fine shrub, thriving well in wet soil.

Azalea arborescens has fragrant, white or rose-tinted flowers, the plant growing from eight to ten feet in height.

Azalea viscosa has flowers from white to rose in color, and grows from four to eight feet high.

Azalea nudiflora grows to a height of from two to six feet; the flowers range in color from white to deep pink and open just before the leaves unfold.

Azalea calendulacea has flowers ranging in color from orange-yellow to red; it grows from four to ten feet high.

Azalea vaseyi attains a height of from five to ten feet, and has beautiful pink flowers.

All the Azaleas like a fine, peaty soil where they will have an abundant supply of water. If planted in swamps they should be raised above the water on low mounds.

Ilex verticillata (Winterberry) is a beautiful, red-berried native shrub that delights in a low, wet position. The bright red berries are borne on the young twigs of the current year's growth, and measure about one-quarter inch across.

Cornus stolonifera (Red-stemmed Dogwood) is a very effective shrub for the water's edge, growing from six to eight feet in height. The leaves are light green above and paler underneath. In winter, the stems of the previous season's growth are of a bright red color. This shrub should be severely cut down every spring so as to encourage a strong growth of young shoots that will take on this beautiful red color the following winter.

Alnus rugosa (A. serrulata) is also well adapted for wet places; it grows from eight to twenty feet high and is perfectly hardy.

Air the trees and shrubs should be so planted and traversed by a walk that one can wander out and in among them. The full extent of the water should never be seen from any one point, but at each turn of the path a fresh view of the pond should break upon the vision. (This is not desirable in the case of ponds of small size, as it would not only minimize the effect but also give a strained, artificial look to the pond). This effect can be easily created by having at some parts steep banks, the tops planted with some of the trees or shrubs already named. At other points the water can be hidden from view by a planting of shrubs only. Always bear in mind that the pond should not be shaded from the South, Southeast, and Southwest; therefore, at these points only the smaller growing trees or shrubs should be used. Where the Rhododendrons thrive well no more beautiful and appropriate subjects can be selected for planting at the water's edge, and a generous collection of both native and hybrid varieties should be employed. In planting the Rhododendrons the native kinds should be grouped; especially should this be done in the case of Rhododendron maximum, as it flowers much later than the hybrids, and it is always well to plant in groups the kinds that bloom at the same time.

The following list of hybrid Rhododendrons furnishes a selection of the best of each color, which will aid intending purchasers: Rhododendron album grandiflorum, white and blush; Rhododendron blandum, white and yellow; Rhododendron blandyanum, bright cherry; Rhododendron everesti-anum, crimpled rosy lilac; Rhododendron General Grant, rosy scarlet; Rhododendron grandiflorum, large rosy crimson; Rhododendron gloriosum, blush, large flowers; Rhododendron perspicuum, clear white; Rhododendron purpureum grandiflorum, showy purple; Rhododendron roseum elegans, rose; Rhododendron caractacus, large truss, rich purple crimson; and Rhododendron Abraham Lincoln, rosy red.

Chapter IV

SOIL

TO grow all Nymphaeas and Nelumbiums successfully they must be supplied with good, rich soil in abundance. Those of the larger growing, night blooming class make a great growth of root and leaves and must be afforded plenty of food in the soil, which should be of sufficient depth to carry them through the season successfully, that they may attain the greatest development of leaf and flower. If the soil is not sufficiently enriched the plant food will soon become exhausted, and the plants will show yellow, starved leaves and small flowers that will be no credit to the grower.

Making the Compost—Fertilizers

For best results, prepare the soil as carefully as you would for roses or any other greenhouse plants. The sod from an old pasture (or from any grass field with a good sod) and soil inclined to a heavy clay texture, is the best for waterlilies. This should be taken to a depth of four inches, and carted to a place where it can be mixed with an equal amount of cow manure, if it can be obtained. If not, use horse manure. The latter, however, is not as good for this class of plants. Also be careful that no pig manure is mixed with the fertilizer, as this will burn the roots badly. Do not accept manure that has been lying outside, exposed to sun and rain for a year or more. Such material as a plant food is then little better than leafmold. Get good, strong, fresh manure, with as little straw in it as possible. Make a layer of soil about six inches in depth, then add a layer of manure of the same depth, and so continue until the pile has reached a height of about four feet, and of whatever length and width are required to furnish the soil necessary to put into the pond. The soil pile should then be covered with boards, or other material, so as to shed rain and ward off the sun's rays. After the soil has been in this condition for some weeks it should be turned over and chopped, mixing the soil and manure thoroughly, afterward throwing it into a pile similar to the first, and covering it in the same way. This process should be repeated three times; the soil will then be ready to place in the boxes, or on the bottom of the pond. The soil can be cut and composted in the fall, or in early spring; it makes very little difference when the work is done, only see to it that the soil and manure are well mixed and that the work is done when the soil is not in an overwet condition.

In preparing soil for this class of plants, as well as for all others, it should not be handled when wet; for in this state the soil will get hard and lumpy, preventing its thorough incorporation with the manure. If cow manure cannot be secured, sheep manure will prove an excellent substitute; but being a much stronger plant food, not more than one part sheep manure to eight parts of soil must be used. When sheep manure is employed, it should not be mixed with the soil until the last turning of the pile. All soils will be benefited by the addition of some ground bonemeal, in small quantities; but it should be "ground bone," not cut with sulphuric acid, which is very injurious to plant growth. Use one-half pound of bonemeal to one cubic foot or 13 ½ pounds to a yard (27 cubic feet) of soil. The bonemeal should be incorporated with the soil at its last turning. The same amount of wood ashes should be added to the soil when it is put into the boxes, or on the pond bottom.

A word of caution as to the use of bonemeal and wood ashes may not be out of place here: These materials should be mixed with the soil as directed, and should not come in contact with each other by applying them simultaneously. If this is done, the potash of the wood ashes will free the ammonia contained in the bonemeal, which will evaporate and be lost. The bonemeal should always be mixed with the soil a few weeks ahead of the application of the wood ashes.

Soil for Seedlings

The soil in which to raise waterlily plants from seed should be a light, sandy loam; or, if this is not available, then a good loam that has not been composted with manure, with the addition of one-third sand, or enough to give the soil the desired open texture. The whole should be passed through a quarter-inch screen. No manure must be used in the soil in which the seed is sown. Manure generally causes fermentation, killing many of the young plants. It should only be used in the soil when the plantlets are ready to be potted off separately into small two-inch pots; then the addition of well-decayed manure will be beneficial and hasten the growth. When the plants are ready for a larger pot, the soil composted for the larger plants will answer, simply passing it through a half-inch screen.

Chapter V

PLANTING AND WINTERING

Planting in Soil on Bottom of Pond

THIS method of planting should be adopted only in large ponds where it will be difficult or impossible to draw off the water. The roots of a number of the lilies, once planted where they have unrestricted room, will very soon spread over the whole pond and intermingle in such a way that the weaker growing kinds will be destroyed by the more robust ones.

In planting roots in large, natural ponds, the roots should be pressed down into the soft mud, two or three inches deep, and held in place by stones until the plants get well rooted. If this is not done, the roots may be disturbed and rise to the surface. The majority of the hardy waterlilies increase very rapidly from the roots, therefore they should have plenty of room between the plants, especially if in a large pond. The stronger growing varieties, such as all the Nymphaea odorata section (with the exception of Nymphaea odorata minor), Nymphaea marliacea rosea, Nymphaea marliacea carnea, Nymphaea marliacea albida, Nymphaea marliacea chromatella, Nymphaea alba, Nymphaea alba candidissima, Nymphaea gladstoniana, with the reniformis (Tuberosa) varieties, should be planted not less than six feet apart, and in the deeper water of the pond. None of the reniformis section should be planted on the bottom of the pond, unless the roots can be confined in an enclosure, formed either of brick or boards, set on edge in the shape of a box.

The medium growing varieties, such as Nymphaea robinsoni, Nymphaea James Brydon and Nymphaea gloriosa can be planted four feet apart, and in water of a depth of eighteen inches.

The weaker growing varieties such as Nymphaea helvola, Nymphaea pygmaea, Nymphaea laydekeri rosea, Nymphaea laydekeri purpurea, Nymphaea andreana, Nymphaea seignoreti, Nymphaea marliacea flammea, Nymphaea marliacea rubra punctata, Nymphaea Arethusa, Nymphaea Aurora, Nymphaea fulva, Nymphaea marliacea lilacea, should be planted close to the edge of the pond in water from twelve to eighteen inches in depth, and from two to three feet between the plants.

The leaf surface of the hardy waterlilies varies with the strength and vigor of the plant. The stronger sorts named above will cover a circle of from six to eight feet in diameter, the medium growers from four to six feet; while the smaller kinds will cover a space of from two to four feet.

The planting of hardy waterlilies can be done at any time from the start of growth in spring, generally about April first, up to the last week of August. While plants set out before or after these dates may do all right, there is a certain amount of danger of losing the roots by a late spring or an early cold fall, retarding the growth.

The tender or tropical waterlilies should not be planted until settled warm weather arrives, or until the temperature of the water reaches 65 or 70 degrees. They should be set out from eight to ten feet apart. The tender night flowering waterlilies are the strongest growers; the leaves of these will cover a circle of from twelve to fifteen feet in diameter. The tender day flowering waterlilies are not quite so vigorous, but will cover a space of from eight to twelve feet. The leaf surface of all waterlilies, however, is governed by the amount of soil and plant food available, that of the very strongest varieties not occupying a space of six feet in diameter unless food and heat conditions are favorable. The tropical lilies will have been in pots for a few weeks, and will have several leaves when they are received from the growers. They should be planted carefully without damaging the ball. If the water is deeper than that in which the plants have been growing, the leaves, at planting, will be entirely submerged. This will have no damaging effect, as generally within a few hours the leaves will be floating on the surface. It is not well to plant any of the lilies in water more than three feet in depth (that is, with that amount of water above the roots) and in that depth only the very strongest growers should be placed. The tender lilies should be planted where they will have the benefit of the direct sunlight all day, if possible.

Planting in Soil in Boxes or Tubs

This is by all means the best method of growing waterlilies, as then they are confined to the space allowed to each one, and the caretaker can walk among the boxes without danger of breaking the plants or stirring up the mud on the bottom of the pond. The size of the boxes, placed four feet apart, should be from two by two feet by one foot deep for the smaller Nymphaeas, such as Nymphaea pygmaea, Nymphaea pygmaea helvola, Nymphaea laydekeri rosea and Nymphaea laydekeri purpurea, Nymphaea laydekeri lucida, Nymphaea andreana, Nymphaea fulva, Nymphaea Arethusa, Nymphaea Aurora, Nymphaea seignoreti, Nymphaea Wm. Falconer, Nymphaea marliacea rubra punctata, Nymphaea marliacea ignea, Nymphaea marliacea flammea, and Nymphaea James Brydon; and for the tender ones, Nymphaea capensis, Nymphaea coerulea, Nymphaea zanzibariensis and its varieties. Up to three by three feet by one foot for the larger growers like gladstoniana, marliacea rosea, etc. These boxes should be six feet apart from center to center. For the tropical lilies, such as Nymphaea omarana, Nymphaea dentata, Nymphaea devoniensis, boxes four by four feet by one foot will be none too large, and they should be eight to ten feet apart from center to center.

If oil barrels are available they can be sawn in two, and will answer very well in place of boxes. These barrels should be burned lightly to remove any oil or other deleterious matter remaining of their former contents; they can then be filled with the soil, and carried to their places in the pond. The lily roots should be planted from two to three inches deep, and the soil covered with one inch of coarse sand or gravel to keep down the manure, and prevent the fish from disturbing the soil in the boxes.

When all the lilies have been planted the water can be turned in and allowed to cover the crowns to the depth of four inches. This quantity of water will be sufficient until the plants begin to grow, when more can be added until the pond is full, care being taken that the plants do not receive a check from too much cold water being admitted at one time. It is better to supply the water in this manner than to fill the pond as soon as planting is done, as, if the latter plan be adopted, there is always danger of losing plants, especially newly divided roots.

The hardy lilies, once planted in boxes, need not be disturbed; all that is required the following spring being to remove the sand, or gravel, and fork in a good top dressing of cow manure, replacing the sand. The year following the boxes should be emptied and refilled with fresh soil and the roots of the lilies divided and planted as before.

Cultural Directions for Aquatics

After the lilies have been planted, their wants are few. All decaying leaves and flowers should be removed as soon as they begin to look unsightly. If scum should gather on the surface of the water, force it toward the overflow pipe by the use of the hose and a good pressure of water, when it can be easily got rid of. Green scum will form whenever new soil and manure have been added to the pond, the still, warm water having a tendency to promote the growth of this particular algae. Should the scum appear in such quantities as to make the pond unsightly, allow a stream of water to flow through the pond for several days, which will soon abate the trouble.

Keep the pond as nearly full of water as possible. If the. water is allowed to get low, and a large quantity of colder water admitted, the temperature in the pond will be lowered in proportion to the additional volume of water supplied. If only hardy lilies are grown in the pond this will make little difference, but tropical lilies thrive best in a temperature as near 80 degrees as possible; therefore, where both hardy and tender lilies are grown in the same pond, the temperature of the water should be maintained at that degree, or as near to it as can be. Keep a sharp lookout for insects and other enemies, never affording them an opportunity to spread before applying proper remedies described in another chapter.

Wintering Tubers and Rhizomes

After a good, sharp frost, the tender lilies should be removed from the pond, and such as are required for winter flowers in the greenhouse tank, or for propagation, should be potted and placed in the tank. The leaves should be removed from the others and the tubers placed under the greenhouse bench, or in some other place where they can be kept cool without danger of being frozen, and away from mice and rats. After a few weeks these roots should be examined, and all the young tubers removed. These look very much like hickory nuts and will be found growing around the old tuber. They can be kept during winter in pots, between layers of damp sand, at a temperature of from 50 to 60 degrees until it is time to start them in the spring. The old tubers of Nymphaea lotus and Nymphaea rubra varieties are of no further use, as they begin to decay as soon as lifted from the pond and should be thrown away after the young tubers are removed. All the zanzibariensis, gracilis, capensis, and coerulea sections should be potted up and placed in water at a temperature as near to 50 degrees as possible. This temperature will keep them in a semi-dormant condition until they are wanted in the spring. If there is no greenhouse tank available in which to place the plants, the tubers can be removed and stored in sand, as described on preceding page.

The roots, or rhizomes, of the hardy lilies need not be removed from the pond if a sufficient depth of water can be maintained above the crowns so that the roots will not be actually frozen. This will have to be determined by personal observation of the thickness of ice formed during the winter. If there is danger of frost reaching the roots a quantity of tree leaves spread over the crowns, kept in place by a sprinkling of sand, or soil, over them, will protect the roots from frost without removal from the pond.

If the lilies have been grown in boxes, or tubs, these can be carried into the cellar or cool greenhouse, and placed under the bench. Whichever method is adopted, care must be taken that the soil does not become dry but is kept in a moist condition. This is essential to carry the roots successfully through the winter. If the roots become dry, they will shrivel; dry rot will result, which soon destroys them. More roots of hardy lilies are lost every winter through being kept too dry than by being frozen. Just how much frost the roots will withstand has not been determined. It may be said that all lilies in the tuberosa, odorata and alba sections will withstand several degrees of frost, which would prove fatal to the Zanzibar and tetragona (pygmaca) section. The same is true of many of Marliac's hybrids.

In cement basins, where there is danger of the walls being cracked by frost, it is well to draw off all the water, and either remove the boxes to the cellar or greenhouse, or fill the basin with tree leaves, placing evergreen branches on top of these. If this method of protection is adopted, some means must be taken to keep rats and mice from the basin, for if allowed access to the lily roots these rodents will soon destroy them, being very partial to the Nymphaea roots during the winter months when other food is scarce.

Chapter VI

HARDY WATERLILIES

THE hardy waterlilies begin to flower very early in the season. In sheltered ponds in the vicinity of New York and Philadelphia the first week of May will see several of them in bloom; and from that time well into September flowers of hardy waterlilies can be picked. The roots of the hardy lilies will commence to flower within a few weeks after planting and keep on blooming throughout the season, so that one has not to wait a whole year for the plants to become established.

The hardy lilies give us a great range and variation in the form of the petals as well as in the color of the blooms. Some of the flowers rise above the water on stems of from six to nine inches; others float on the surface, presenting an endless variety in leaf and flower. The best of the hardy lilies spring from the American species, Nymphaea odorata, Nymphaea reniformis (Tuberosa), and the Mexican variety, Nymphaea mexicana. These, with the European species, Nymphaea alba and Nymphaea alba rubra, and the Chinese Nymphaea tetragona (pygmaea), have all been used by the hybridist to give us the many beautiful forms we now possess. Nymphaea odorata, the white fragrant pondlily of the Eastern States, is still a desirable one, and should be grown by every person who cultivates waterlilies. It delights in deep, rich soil. The flower is white, in size from three to five inches across, with golden yellow stamens; the sepals and tips of the petals are very often tinted pink. The flowers are very fragrant. The leaves are dark green on the upper side while the underside is a reddish green.

A large number of hybrids and chance seedlings from Nymphaea odorata are now in cultivation. The best of these are Nymphaea odorata luciana, a variety of great beauty and vigorous growth; the flowers measure from three to six inches across, and are of a beautiful rosy pink color.

In Nymphaea odorata caroliniana we have a natural hybrid and a very beautiful one. The flowers are of a delicate rose flesh color, while the stamens are clear yellow. The plant is of strong growth, with large leaves which often measure twelve inches in diameter.

NYMPHAEA COMANCHE
Of a rich apricot color, becoming a coppery orange
as the flower ages

Nymphaea Conqueror is a free growing hybrid of that well known raiser of new lilies, M. Latour-Marliac. It is of robust growth and free flowering habit. The flower is of deep pink color, shading to deep purplish-pink. The petals are broad, incurving tips, reflexed, giving the flower a distinct cup shape. The stamens are numerous and yellow in color.

Nymphaea Attraction. One of the finest of recent French introductions. The flowers measure eight inches in diameter. On first opening the flowers are a garnet red with almost white sepals and yellow stamens, lightly touched with mahogany. As the flower reaches maturity the color deepens until the flowers become dark red and the sepals streaked with garnet.

The flowers are readily distinguishable on the water, being so bright and attractive.

Nymphaea Colossea. A remarkably fine flower of large size having a long period of bloom. Except in size, resembling somewhat N. marliacea rosea.

Nymphaea Comanche. Flowers are large, of a rich apricot color, on opening becoming a dark coppery-orange streaked with glowing red as the flower ages. The foliage is an attractive olive green flaked wth brown; one of the best lilies of recent introduction.

Nymphaea Escarboucle. The color is an intense vermilion shade, of uniform color throughout the petals A very free bloomer and vigorous in growth.

Nymphaea odorata exquisita produces flowers of an intense rosecarmine color.

NYMPHAEA ESCARBOUCLE
An intense vermilion colored flower

Nymphaca odorata gigantea, from the Southern United States, gives large, pure white flowers from four to seven inches across. The leaves are large, deep green, with the underside generally tinted purplish at the margin; very free flowering.

Nymphaea Eugenia de Land. A seedling from one of the odorata group. Flowers are extra large, of the true N. odorata type; petals long and lanceolate; color a deep rose pink of iridescent hue. A vigorous and free flowering variety. Flowers float on the surface of the water.

NYMPHAEA EUGENIA DE LAND
A large flowering, deep rose pink, hardy waterlily

Nymphaea formosa. A large flowering variety, clear pink with broad incurving petals; flowers very freely. One of the finest pink lilies in cultivation.

Nymphaea odorata minor produces small, fragrant white flowers, from two to three inches across. This lily is much used for growing in tubs and for planting at the edges of ponds.

In Nymphaea odorata rosea we have the far-famed Cape Cod pink waterlily. The flowers, about four inches in diameter, are of a beautiful rose pink color at the tips of the petals, deepening to intense pink at the center of the flower. The stamens are pure yellow. The flowers of this Nymphaea are very fragrant; the leaves are dark reddish green on both sides.

Nymphaea odorata sulphurea is a hybrid between Nymphaea odorata and Nymphaea mexicana. The flowers measure from four to five inches across, are of a deep sulphur yellow color, rising above the water to a height of from three to six inches. The leaves are blotched with brown spots and float on the surface of the pond.

A large flowering variety of the preceding is Nymphaea odorata sulphurea grandiflora. This lily is larger in flower and leaf; otherwise it is identical with Nymphaea odorata sulphurea.

Nymphaea Pink Opal. A very fine odorata seedling. The color is an attractive, deep pink, medium-sized flower. It is one of the finest pink lilies for cut flower purposes.

Nymphaea odorata W. B. Shaw is a seedling from the beautiful Nymphaea odorata caroliniana. The plant flowers as freely as that well-known variety. The color of the flower is much deeper and brighter than that of the parent.

Nymphaea Mrs. Richmond. This is a very fine variety of recent introduction. The flowers attain a size of nine inches in diameter; in color, pale pink, deeper at the base of the petals, which are quite broad with deep yellow stamens. The petals are slightly incurved, giving the flower an attractive cup-shaped form.

The well known Nymphaea tuberosa (reniformis) is another of our native species. It has deep green leaves, some of which stand out of the water to a height of twelve inches when crowded. It is one of the strongest growing lilies, and should not be planted, unless the roots can be confined;

NYMPHAEA ODORATA W. B. SHAW

even then it will soon spread all over the pond by means of its seed. It bears pure white flowers, from four to nine inches in diameter, with broad petals. The plant is only moderately free flowering, and not so desirable for cultivation as some of the others.

Nymphaea Rose Arey. A seedling from odorata, very free flowering and of strong growth. The flowers are large, up to eight inches in diameter, very sweet scented; the color is a bright cerise pink.

Nymphaea tuberosa rosea is not quite so vigorous in growth as its parent, but it produces more flowers, the color of which is a light shade of flesh pink. They rise above the water from two to three inches.

Nymphaea tuberosa richardsoni is one of the finest of the hardy lilies, with pure white flowers, very double, and of large size, from six to eight inches across. The plant has the vigorous growth of the type. While it is one of the hardy lilies indispensable in every collection, it gives few flowers for the amount of space it occupies.

NYMPHAEA ALBA

Nymphaea tuberosa rubra is a hybrid of beautiful rosy red color with red stamens; the flowers are from five to seven inches across, with the delicate perfume of the odorata section. The plant is of strong, vigorous growth. This is quite a desirable variety, but not very free flowering.

Nymphaea alba is the well-known white lily from Europe. The flowers float on the water, and measure from four to six inches across. The plant blooms very freely and is of quick, strong growth.

Nymphaea alba candidissima is a large, free flowering white variety of strong vigorous growth. The flowers are much larger than those of Nymphaea alba. The leaves are large and deep green. The plant blooms continuously throughout the season.

In Nymphaea marliacea albida we have a pure white flower of large size with yellow stamens and quite fragrant. The sepals are tinted pink. The plant is of free growth, and blooms continuously the whole season. The leaves are large, deep green above, the underside being deep red in the young stage. This is one of the best white waterlilies in cultivation for all purposes.

NYMPHAEA MARLIACEA ALBIDA

NYMPHAEA MARLIACEA CHROMATELLA

Nymphaea marliacea rosea is still one of the best of the deep pink hardy lilies, and a fitting companion to the preceding. The flowers are of large size, deep rose pink in color. The plant is very free flowering, and of strong, vigorous growth, with large leaves which are purplish red in the young state changing to deep green. This is one of the choicest waterlilies.

In Nymphaea marliacea carnea we have a lily similar to the last named in flower, leaf and growth of plant. The color is a soft flesh pink, deeper toward the center of the flower. The bloom exhales a sweet vanilla fragrance. The plant is very free flowering.

Nymphaea marliacea chromatella has charming canary yellow flowers, from four to six inches in diameter, with bright yellow stamens. The leaves are beautifully mottled with brown. The plant flowers freely, and is of easy, quick growth. When it has remained undisturbed for some years the leaves become crowded and rise above the water at the center of the plant to a height of twelve inches, thus hiding a large number of the flowers.

NYMPHAEA GLADSTONIANA

To avoid this the plant should be divided every two years. This is, at the present writing, the best yellow hardy waterlily in cultivation for all purposes.

In Nymphaea Wm. Doogue we have a fine lily of delicate coloring. The flowers are large, of a soft shell pink color, with pink sepals, which are very wide and slightly incurving, giving a beautiful cup-shaped bloom. The plant flowers freely the whole season.

Nymphaea gladstoniana is a fine lily of beautiful form and strong, robust growth. It requires plenty of space for its best development at both root and top. The flowers are of the purest white, cup-shaped, with golden yellow stamens and very large. The plant blooms freely. The leaves are dark green, the leaf stalk being striped brown as in Nymphaea tuberosa. The plant is also inclined to push the leaves above the water.

With Nymphaea laydckeri rosea we come to a distinct class of hybrids, raised by M. Latour-Marliac, of Temple-sur-Lot, France, who has given us many beautiful and interesting hybrid waterlilies. This lily is of the form of Nymphaea pygmaea (tetragona) which it resembles in many ways, but not in the color and size of the flowers. On first opening the bloom is of a soft shell pink, which as it gets older becomes deep carmine rose. The stamens are orange red. The plant is moderate in growth, but very free flowering, and is desirable for tubs and small pools, or for planting at the edge of a pond or tank.

Nymphaea laydekeri lilacea gives fragrant flowers of a soft rose-lilac color, shaded bright carmine, with yellow stamens. The leaves are bright glossy green beautifully blotched with brown.

Nymphaea laydekeri purpurea produces flowers of a carmine rose color, darker toward the center. The center petals and sepals are of a bright rose and the stamens orange red. The plant flowers freely and continuously the whole season.

Nymphaea laydekeri fulgens throws flowers of a brilliant crimson magenta color, with garnet rose stamens. Blooms are nicely cup-shaped.

Nymphaea lucida has flowers of a rosy vermilion color, darker in the center, with orange stamens. The leaves are beautifully blotched with reddish brown. The plant is very free in flower and growth.

Nymphaea fulva gives flowers of a bright yellow color, with a red overlay, the general color being a bright carmine purple.

Nymphaea andreana produces flowers of a dark red color shaded with yellow. The leaves are blotched with chestnut brown. The plant blooms freely and is a very desirable variety.

Nymphaea Aurora gives flowers of a soft rosy yellow when first opening, changing to deep red as the flower gets older.

Nymphaea seignoreti has a medium sized flower, pale yellow in color shaded with pink and carmine, with orange yellow stamens. The blooms rise above the water to a height of six inches. The leaves are beautifully spotted with brown. This variety is free in flower.

Nymphaea Arethusa gives a bright crimson pink flower of large size. The plant flowers very freely.

In Nymphaea James Brydon we have a very fine hardy lily, one of the freest in flower and growth, and in every particular one of the most desirable of its class. The flowers measure from five to six inches across; the petals are broad, concave and incurving, giving a flower of a fine cup-shape. The color is a rich rosy crimson, while on the reverse of the petals is a silvery sheen. This variety is well adapted either for growing in tubs, boxes, or planted out in the pond.

NYMPHAEA JAMES BRYDON

Nymphaea Wm. Falconer is the darkest colored of all the hardy waterlilies in cultivation. The flowers measure from six to seven inches across, are of a bright garnet ruby color, with yellow stamens. The leaves are dark red when first unfolding, changing to deep green with red veins as the leaf reaches maturity. This variety is shy in flowering, otherwise it is excellent.

Nymphaea gloriosa is a magnificent variety with flowers from four to six inches across of beautiful form, which float on the water. They are of a deep carmine rose color, becoming deep red with age. The plant is very free in flower, blooming continuously throughout the season. This lily is the best of this class for all purposes.

Nymphaea robinsoni gives a fine flower of a unique coloring; the ground color is yellow with an overlay of purplish red; the general tone being a dark orange red. The plant is very free in flower and growth, with dark green leaves spotted with brown above and dark red on the underside. This is one of the best, and should be grown by all who have a collection of hardy waterlilies.

NYMPHAEA GLORIOSA

Nymphaea marliacea ignea produces flowers from four to five inches across of a deep carmine color with cardinal stamens. The leaves are of a rich bronze when young, changing with age to deep green with brown blotches.

Nymphaea marliacea flammea has large flowers of amaranth red, shaded with white. The stamens are deep orange. The leaves are green much blotched with chestnut brown.

Nymphaea flava is a pale yellow waterlily from our Southland. The flowers measure from three to four inches across, rising out of the water from three to six inches. The leaves are dark green, blotched with brown.

Nymphaea mexicana gives a bright canary yellow flower from four to five inches across, with golden yellow stamens. The leaves are small, much spotted with brown on the surface, the underside dark crimson brown with black spots. This is a free and continuous bloomer and is perfectly hardy at Philadelphia. This lily and Nymphaea flava may winterkill farther north.

Nymphaea pygmaea (tetragona) is the smallest Nymphaea in cultivation. The flowers are white with yellow stamens, from one and one-half to two and one-half inches across. They exhale a tea fragrance. The plant is free in flower. The leaves are dark green with occasional brown spots, the underside being reddish green.

Nymphaea pygmaea helvola is the result of a cross between Nymphaea pygmaea and Nymphaea mexicana. It gives beautiful small yellow flowers which float on the surface of the water. They are about two inches in diameter. The leaves are small, beautifully mottled with brown spots, the underside of a reddish green color. The plant flowers freely and is well adapted for tub culture or for planting in shallow water at the edge of the pond.

Nymphaea alba rubra is the true Swedish red waterlily; a beautiful flower where it thrives well but, unfortunately, the water in nearly all our ponds is too warm for it, hence it is very rare in America. It should be grown in a pond, or pool, fed with cold spring water. The color of the flowers is rosy carmine with orange stamens.

SELECTIONS OF THE BEST HARDY WATERLILIES

The best six hardy lilies for all purposes should include the following: Nymphaea marliacea albida, white; Nymphaea marliacea rosea, pink; Nymphaea marliacea chromatella, yellow; Nymphaea Attraction, garnet red; Nymphaea odorata Rose Arey, rose pink; Nymphaea robinsoni, orange red.

The best twelve should include the foregoing with the following additional six: Nymphaea gladstoniana, white; Nymphaea Wm. Falconer, red; Nymphaea Mrs. Richardson, carmine rose; Nymphaea W. B. Shaw, bright rose pink; Nymphaea alba candidissima, white; Nymphaea tuberosa richardsoni, white.

The best eighteen would include all of the above with the addition of Nymphaea lucida, rosy vermilion; Nymphaea odorata luciana, rosy pink; Nymphaea odorata, white; Nymphaea fulva, yellow shaded pink; Nymphaea Wm. Doogue, soft shell pink; Nymphaea odorata rosea, rose pink. The best of the small flowered forms are: Nymphaea pygmaea, white; Nymphaea pygmaea helvola, yellow; Nymphaea mexicana, yellow; Nymphaea laydekeri rosea, rose pink; Nymphaea seignoreti, yellow shaded pink and carmine; Nymphaea odorata minor, white.

NYMPHAEA MARLIACEA ROSEA

Chapter VII

NELUMBIUMS

THEIR DESIRABILITY IN THE WATER GARDEN

NELUMBIUMS, or Sacred Lotus as they are more commonly named, form one of the most interesting classes of plants in the vegetable kingdom. They always command interest and admiration because of the plant's sacred history and its beautiful, large flowers, which are borne on tall stems towering above the stately silvery bluish green leaves that often measure from two to two feet six inches in diameter, borne on stems from three to eight feet in height. The grand foliage, aside from its magnificent flowers, well repays one for growing the Lotus. The Nelumbiums begin to bloom toward the end of June and continue to flower well into August. The flowers, like those of the Nymphaeas, open for three successive days. The first day they never open full, but just enough to give one a glimpse of their beautiful, silk-like stamens; the blooms quickly close, opening again the following morning, quite full, and remain open for several hours, then they close to open out quite flat the next day, when the petals begin to fall.

The Nelumbiums are of quick growth, and if good sized roots are planted they will flower the first season, if the location is congenial. If, however, they do not bloom the first year, they are sure to do so the following one.

The flowers are of beautiful colors, of large size, exhaling a delicate perfume. The plants bloom freely when once established, and are perfectly hardy as long as the roots are below the frost line or are not exposed to actual freezing.

The Nelumbium is a native of India, and was held sacred by the Hindus. It was early introduced into Egypt and the Egyptians made use of the seeds for food. The seeds were gathered, dried in the sun, and pounded into a fine meal which was then baked into bread. The American Indians utilize the seeds of the American yellow Lotus, Nelumbium luteum, in a similar manner. The Chinese and Japanese still eat the seeds and roots of the plant, which are offered for sale in their stores at the present time.

The Nelumbium speciosum was introduced into America by E. D. Sturtevant, of Bordentown, N. J., about 1876. A year or two later he set out one plant in the open which grew so luxuriantly that in eight years a space of three-quarters of an acre was covered with a mass of flowers and foliage. From that time on the Nelumbium has grown in popular favor and has been planted extensively in all parts of America.

In Boxes Submerged in Pond

Its planting is by no means restricted to large places only; many an amateur has his Lotus growing in a half barrel in his yard, and the Nelumbium can be cultivated very successfully in this way, if no better accommodation is available.

To carry the roots of Nelumbiums safely through the winter they should not be disturbed in the fall or winter months, and, if possible, should remain in the pond or basin throughout the winter. If the roots are planted in the soil on the bottom of the pond, they will be deep down in the soil out of reach of the frost; if in boxes or half barrels in the pond, or basin, the roots will be down on the bottom of the receptacle and therefore out of reach of the frost, unless ice forms to the bottom of the pond. If this should happen the boxes should be removed to a cellar where there will be no danger of the roots being frozen.

The Nelumbiums are strong, robust growing plants which require a large amount of space, soil and food for their proper development. The soil recommended for the Nymphaeas will suit the requirements of Nelumbiums as well.

To obtain the best results in growing Nelumbiums, they should have a basin to themselves where the roots will be allowed to run at will. Nelumbiums throw out roots a distance of fifteen feet in a single season, with leaves at every joint, generally about eighteen inches apart; therefore, in a very short time all other growths in a pond with them will be killed. If it is not practicable to devote a basin to the Lotus, then a part of the pond, or basin, should be boarded up in the form of a box, of whatever shape and size desired. This should be of sufficient depth to reach to the bottom of the pond. If the bottom is of concrete the box should rest on it allowing the edge of the box to extend above the level of the soil at least six inches. This will keep the floating runners (roots) within the confines of the box and prevent them getting over the edge. In making boxes for Nelumbiums the corners should be filled in with a piece of wood, so cut that it will turn the roots aside and prevent them being jammed into the corners where they would be injured.

The best time to plant the Lotus is in the spring, when settled warm weather has arrived, which will be, generally, about the second week in May in the Northern States. At this time the roots receive very little check by removal, as the warm temperature starts the plants into growth at once allowing little chance for the roots to decay, which they are likely to do if kept dormant for any length of

ROOT OR RHIZOME OF NELUMBIUM
Showing three growing points. In planting great care should be taken not to break the point or the plant will die

time after being removed. If, for some unavoidable reason, planting has to be deferred to a later date, then plants that have been started into growth in pots or pans should be procured in preference to rhizomes.

In planting the roots care should be taken not to break the growing point, which would render the tuber useless; should this happen, it may then be thrown away, unless there is another growing point on the root, which is rarely the case. The roots should be planted in the soil in a horizontal position and covered to a depth of six inches with a coating of two inches of gravel, or coarse sand over the soil, as recommended in the case of Nymphaeas.

Grown in Boxes or Half Barrels

Another method of growing the Lotus is to plant it in boxes or half barrels, and submerge them in the basin, treating them in the same way as recommended for the Nymphaeas. So handled the boxes can be moved around the basin at will and placed where the plants will provide the best effect; the roots are confined within the boxes and there is therefore little danger of them escaping. If planted in this manner boxes four feet by four feet by one foot will be found a good size for all the Lotus. An oil barrel sawn in two and burned out to get rid of the adhering oil will furnish a suitable receptacle for the growth of these plants; not being as large as the boxes previously described, these half barrels are more easily moved around the basin. The boxes, or half barrels, should be overhauled every two years. The receptacles should be filled with fresh soil as recommended for Nymphaea culture, and three or four roots allowed for each box or barrel. The following spring all the work required will be to remove the top soil and afford a good rich top dressing of cow manure, with a little soil on top, finishing with a layer of sand or gravel.

Grown in Tubs on the Lawn

Nelumbiums are also grown extensively in tubs or half barrels placed on the lawn. The tub is filled with soil to within six inches of the top, the tuber planted, and the remaining space in the tub filled with water. All that is necessary afterward is to replace the water lost by evaporation or seepage, and to see that the tub is emptied at least every two years and fresh soil added. It is also desirable to have one or two gold fish in each barrel to destroy the mosquito larvae that would otherwise hatch there. In lieu of the fish a small quantity of kerosene oil, just sufficient to cover the water with a thin film, can be put into each barrel once a week; this will kill all the larvae without injury to the plants.

Nelumbium speciosum is the well-known, so-called Egyptian Lotus; it throws beautiful flowers about twelve inches across, of a deep rose color on opening the first day, becoming paler as the flower gets older, until the third day when the color is creamy white at the base and center of the petals, the edge tinted light rose pink. The plant has large leaves, deep green above, light silvery green on the reverse. It grows and flowers freely.

NELUMBIUM PEKINENSIS RUBRUM
The best of the deep colored Nelumbiums

NELUMBIUM ROSEUM PLENUM

In Nelumbium pekinensis rubrum we have the best of the deep colored Nelumbiums. The growth of plant and leaves is magnificent, the flowers are very large, of a bright rose carmine color, the petals somewhat reflexed as in Nelumbium speciosum, which this plant resembles very much in habit. It flowers freely and is very desirable.

A double form of the preceding is Nelumbium pekinensis rubrum flore pleno, resembling the parent in color of flowers and habit of plant, but differing from it in the number of petals. The flowers are very double, and are borne on strong stems well above the foliage.

Nelumbium roseum gives flowers of a deep rose pink color, free in growth and flower.

Nelumbium roseum plenum is another double form with bright rose colored blooms; very free in growth and flower.

Nelumbium album grandiflorum, sometimes called Nelumbium album floribunda, gives a fine pure white flower of large size and delicate fragrance. The leaves are large and deep green in color. This is the best white Lotus for all purposes.

Nelumbium album striatum is a variety of the preceding, with all its good qualities. The flowers are fragrant, white, with the petals striped and tipped rosy carmine. The plant is of vigorous growth and free in flower.

NELUMBIUM PEKINENSIS RUBRUM FLORE PLENO

Nelumbium kermesinum produces flowers of a bright pink color, lighter than tfrose of Nelumbium pekinensis rubrum; is free in flower and of easy cultivation.

Nelumbium Shiroman is a magnificent variety, giving large double flowers; on first opening they are cream colored with a few of the petals tinted a light green; as the flower gets older the color fades to pure white. This is a strong, robust plant, flowering as freely as Nelumbium speciosum. The blooms last well in the cut state.

NELUMBIUM SHIROMAN
A magnificent variety, giving large, double flowers

Nelumbium Osiris is a beautiful cup-shaped blossom of deep rose color, strong in growth and free in flower.

Nelumbium pygmaea alba is a dwarf, miniature, white flowered variety, truly a pygmaea in all its parts. The leaves never grow more than eighteen inches above the water. It is very useful for tub cultivation, or for planting at the edge of the pond, where a dwarf subject is desired.

Nelumbium luteum, the native American Lotus, is a beautiful yellow flowered species found growing wild in the Eastern and Central States of America. It is perfectly hardy, of easy culture, succeeding best where planted out in soil on the bottom of the pond.

Chapter VIII

HEATING THE TROPICAL LILY BASIN

HAVING located a basin on the lawn, near the dwelling house, it can be heated from the boiler used in the dwelling during the winter months, thus enabling one to grow the tropical lilies in the Northern States. All that is necessary is to place valves on the flow and return pipes near the boiler, so that the circulation can be regulated at will both as regards the house and the lily basin. A flow pipe can be taken from the boiler and run through a terra cotta pipe to the basin, which should enter about six inches below the water level. The return pipe should be taken through the wall of the basin near the bottom and back to the boiler in the same manner, and in the same trench as the flow pipe. This will insure a free circulation of the water.

There are two methods of heating a lily basin with hot water—one by running pipes all around the basin, thus heating the water by contact with the pipes; the other, to use the basin as a large expansion tank, the flow pipe entering the basin a few inches below the water level, and the return pipe running from the side opposite to that in which the flow enters, so as to insure a proper circulation and mixing of the water.

The first mentioned method is the better of the two, but the more expensive, owing to the amount of pipe required. This will be described first: If it is decided to use the boiler located in the cellar of the dwelling house for heating the pond, the flow pipe, if possible, should be graded so that the highest point will be at the boiler and a gradual fall secured all the way to the basin. Near the boiler, at the highest point, means should be taken to carry off all air that may accumulate there. This can be done by a pipe running to the expansion tank connected with the system, or a pet-cock can be used, which will have to be opened by hand to allow the air to escape, failing which circulation will be stopped. The flow pipes should enter the basin a few inches below the water level, at which point a tee can be placed from which branches can be run around the sides of the basin, grading them so that they will have a fall to the far end (12 inches in 100 feet will be

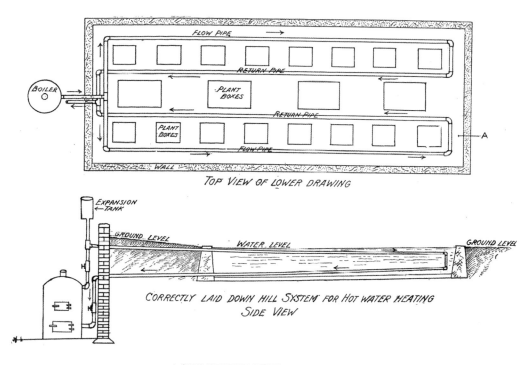

TOP VIEW OF LOWER DRAWING

CORRECTLY LAID DOWN HILL SYSTEM FOR HOT WATER HEATING
SIDE VIEW

A SUGGESTION FOR A HEATED POOL
The above diagrams show the method of laying the pipes and arrangement for the boiler connection. The upper diagram also shows the position of the boxes in which the waterlilies are to be grown

ample) whence they can be returned, grading them with a fall to the boiler, either immediately underneath or a few feet from the flow, which will give a more uniform temperature and a more even distribution of the heat. The size of the pipe used will depend on the size of the basin. For very large basins a flow pipe of three or four inches will be necessary, which can be run to the basin, and then several branches of two-inch pipe run through the water. A pipe of similar size will answer for the return. The amount of radiation necessary to heat a basin to 90 degrees is, approximately, one square foot of heating surface to every 100 to 125 gallons of water. To ascertain how many gallons of water are to be heated, measure the depth, length and width of the basin in cubic feet, add the results, and multiply by 7½, which will give the number of gallons the basin contains; then allow one square foot of radiating surface to every 100 to 125 gallons of water.

For the second method it is necessary to find the number of cubic feet of water contained in the basin and the temperature to which the water has to be raised during the coldest weather, which will be, approximately, 50 degrees. Assuming the water in the tank to be 40 degrees, and desiring to raise it to 90 degrees, find the number of cubic feet of water in the basin which multiply by 62½, the weight in pounds of a cubic foot of water. The result is then to be multiplied by the number of degrees it is desired to raise the water, which was taken as 50 degrees; this will give the heat units which must be imparted to the water by the fire. Under ordinary conditions, boilers of good construction now on the market will radiate not less than 7,500 heat units per pound of coal burned. Ordinary boilers will consume six pounds of coal per square foot of grate surface per hour, with good economy. It is necessary, therefore, to find how many heat units it is desired to impart to the water; this divided by 45,000 will give the number of square feet of grate surface required in the boiler to heat the basin.

The flow pipe in this instance will be graded so as to have a rise from the boiler to the basin, which it will enter a few inches below the water level and stop just inside the wall of the basin. A strainer of gauze wire should be connected to the end of the pipe so as to prevent all foreign substances entering it. This strainer should be of large size; for a three-inch pipe a strainer of from six to eight inches diameter will be required; other sizes in proportion. The flow pipe should have a valve to be closed when cleaning the boiler, otherwise the basin would be emptied. The return pipe should be laid from the side of the basin opposite that in which the flow enters, so as to insure the proper circulation and the mixing of the water. The return, likewise, should be protected by a strainer, and can be run in the same trench with the flow, but should have a good fall back to the boiler. A fall of one foot in a hundred will be ample for both flow and return pipes. Near the boiler, on the return pipe, a valve should be placed and a mud drum, which can be easily cleaned of any sediment deposited, which otherwise would reach the boiler. A very satisfactory arrangement for a mud receptacle is to place a tee on the pipe near the boiler, which can be increased, by the use of reducers, to take a much larger pipe. A piece of pipe about twelve inches in length will answer; this can be closed on the lower end by a cap that can be easily removed to clean out any sediment lodging there.

If this latter method of heating be adopted, it is well to have a boiler that can be easily cleaned, as in nearly all lily basins there is at all times more or less mud in suspension which will be carried

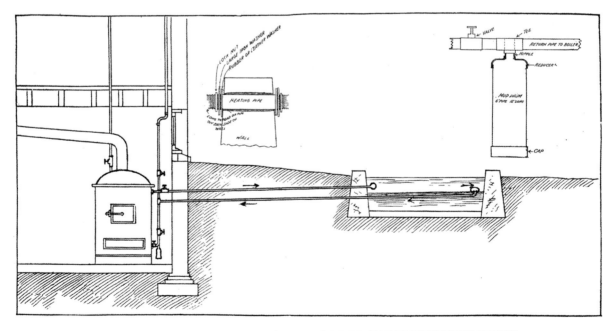

HEATING A POOL OR BASIN FROM THE BOILER OF THE DWELLING HOUSE

The sketch herewith shows how a basin on the lawn may be heated from a hot water boiler in the dwelling house, using the basin as an expansion tank. This is called the open system of heating. Where this method is adopted, a mud-drum, a design of an inexpensive and effective form of which is show at the upper right-hand corner of this diagram, should be placed near the boiler on the return pipe and just below it

In this sketch is also pictured a device demonstrating how to secure a tight joint where the heating pipe passes through a brick or cement wall

These illustrations, with the text, give a clear idea of the neccessary connections and attachments to the boiler. The quantity of mud in the water depends on how the plants are grown. If in boxes, and the soil in these is covered with a good layer of sand, there should be very little muddy water. On the other hand, if the lilies are planted in soil on the bottom of the basin, and the caretaker has to walk around among them, then considerable mud will find its way to the boiler in the course of time.

If steam is available for heating the water, all that is required is a pipe to circle the basin, with small openings in the pipe, every four feet, through which the steam may percolate. One must be certain, however, that the weight or pressure of water in the pool is not greater than the pressure of the steam or the apparatus will not work.

As all basins are heated in order to give a temperature in which the tropical lilies will thrive well, a word as to temperature may not be out of place here. The best results are obtained when a temperature of 80 to 90 degrees can be maintained. A good average will be 85 degrees. In this temperature the Victoria regia can be planted early in May, should reach the blooming stage early in July, and from that date until late fall will be in continuous flower. The other tropical lilies will reach maturity before the Victoria and will keep up a succession of flowers until killed by frost. Hence, in heating a lily basin, one can be assured of nearly six weeks' gain in the spring, and of several weeks' protracted flowering in the fall. If the Victoria is not to be grown in the basin, a temperature of 75 to 80 degrees will be sufficient for the other tender varieties.

A few facts in regard to heating surface of pipes of various sizes may be of interest. To secure one hundred square feet of heating surface in

1 inch pipe it will be necessary to use 290¼ lineal feet.

1¼ inch pipe it will be necessary to use 230 lineal feet.

1½ inch pipe it will be necessary to use 201 lineal feet.

2 inch pipe it will be necessary to use 161 lineal feet.

2½ inch pipe it will be necessary to use 132⅔ lineal feet.

3 inch pipe it will be necessary to use 109 lineal feet.

4 inch pipe it will be necessary to use 84¼ lineal feet.

Approximate length of pipe per square foot heating surface:

1 inch	3 lineal feet.
1¼ inches	2 ft. 4 in.
1½ inches	2 ft.
2 inches	1 ft. 8 in.
2½ inches	1 ft. 4 in.
3 inches	1 ft. 1 in.
4 inches	1 ft.

One square foot of grate surface will supply 200 to 250 square feet of radiation surface. A two-inch pipe will supply 200 to 300, and a three-inch pipe 600 to 800 square feet of radiation.

Chapter IX

TENDER OR TROPICAL WATERLILIES

DAY FLOWERING

OF the tender or tropical waterlilies there are two distinct classes—one flowering during the day, the other during the night. The day flowering ones open their blossoms in the early morning hours and they remain open until afternoon.

To this section belongs Nymphaea gigantea from Australia, the finest of all the day blooming blue lilies. The flowers are of the largest size and delicate in color, which is a soft purplish blue, shading to white at the base of the petals. The stamens are very slender, of a soft yellow, slightly incurving, and quite distinct from those of all other Nymphaeas. The flowers are borne on fine, stiff stems well above the water. The leaves are green above, purplish on the underside. This plant requires for its fullest development a temperature of 80 to 90 degrees with plenty of root room. It should never be subjected to a check from any cause. If the temperature of the water in the basin be allowed to fall several degrees, and to remain for any length of time below the figures given, the plants are likely to go to rest, and may remain dormant the remainder of the season; there-fore, they should never be allowed to become pot-bound, or be subjected to sudden changes of temperature.

Nymphaea Mrs. Edwards Whitaker is a new hybrid waterlily, the result of a cross between N. ovalifolia and N. castaliflora. raised by G. H. Pring, of the Missouri Botanical Garden. This new lily is one of the largest of the day flowering class. The flowers are lavender-blue on first opening, getting paler as the flower ages, closing almost pure white. The flowers often measure ten inches in diameter and last on the plant in good condition for several days. The leaves are almost round, beautifully mottled or streaked with dark red, the underside blotched with purple on a pale green base. One of the remarkable features of this lily is that the flowers open about 6:30 a.m., not closing until about 7:30 p.m. No other lily remains open for so long a period.

Next in order of merit in this class is Nymphaea zanzibariensis. This is the true royal purple waterlily of Africa and still ranks as the best dark blue waterlily in cultivation. It is extremely free in flower and growth. The plant sets seeds freely, but very rarely do the seedlings develop to the true deep purple color of the type; therefore, a plant should be procured from some dealer in aquatics in the spring, and, if planted out, will make a tuber that season which can be easily

NYMPHAEA MRS. EDWARDS WHITAKER

carried through the winter, forming a nice subject for the next season's planting. The surface of the leaves is deep green, the reverse being green and violet; they are from eight to fifteen inches in diameter. The flowers measure from five to ten inches across; the petals are deep blue, sepals green on the outside, purplish blue on the inner side. The stamens are very numerous, dark crimson violet on the outer surface. The flowers are very fragrant. The plant is free in flower, blooming continuously throughout the season.

NYMPHAEA ZANZIBARIENSIS ROSEA
Tender Day Flowering

There are two other forms of this Nymphaea: zanzibariensis azurea, and zanzibariensis rosea; both are similar to the type in everything but the color of the flowers. The bloom of Nymphaea zanzibariensis azurea is of a delicate azure blue, while that of Nymphaea zanzibariensis rosea varies in color, different plants giving from light rose to deep rose colored flowers.

Another delicate light azure blue flower is Nymphaea elegans, from Mexico and Texas. The blooms are of medium size, rarely exceeding more than three to four inches across. The color is a white ground overlaid with light blue. The stamens are yellow tipped with light blue. The leaves are long and narrow, green spotted chocolate brown. This is a beautiful flower, of dainty color, the plants blooming continuously from early in the season until cut down by frost.

Nymphaea coerulea, often named Nymphaea stellata, is the blue Lotus of the Nile, which was held sacred by the Egyptians. The petals are light blue above, dull white below, long and narrow; the sepals are greenish white on the face, the reverse striped and spotted brown. The stamens are yellow. The leaves are light green, with brown spots which fade to green as the leaves age; the underside is green with dark purplish blotches, the edge tinted reddish purple. The flowers measure from three to six inches across and have long conical pointed buds. The plant blooms freely.

NYMPHAEA GIGANTEA VAR. HUDSONIANA

Nymphaea gigantea var. hudsoniana was raised some years ago at Gunnersbury House, England. It is one of the freest in growth and bloom of this favorite lily. The color is a rich deep blue (the inner petals a lighter shade), cup-shaped flower of large size, with beautiful golden stamens. Without doubt, it is the best one of the giganteas. It is easily injured by a sudden check, but where it can be given a heated pool, it will well repay a little extra care.

Nymphaea castaliaflora (Pring) is the result of the intercrossing, by insects, of two varieties of Nymphaea capensis, and by careful selection and self-pollination a variety that will reproduce itself true from seed has been obtained, if the flowers are guarded from foreign pollen. The flowers are large, slightly cup-shaped, petals numerous, and the color of the stamens a fine pink shade. The flowers measure from eight to ten inches across and are very fragrant and open early and close late in the evening. The leaves are light green, mottled brown above and shaded pink underneath.

Nymphaea Mrs. Woodrow Wilson is a new hybrid of the day flowering class, raised by that well-known waterlily specialist, the late William Tricker, of Arlington, New Jersey. It is interesting because the viviparous habit of one of its parents, N. daubeniana, has been transmitted to it; therefore it can be propagated from the plants formed at the junction of the leaf and petiole. The color is lavender-blue, the flower seven to eight inches across, the stamens yellow, tipped with lavender.

Nymphaea Panama-Pacific is a very fine flowering variety of the viviparous group. The buds are bronzy-green, spotted with reddish-brown. On first opening the flowers are a rich, rosy-red; when fully open the color is a distinct reddish-purple with yellow stamens. This variety is highly recommended for greenhouse culture; especially satisfactory as a winter bloomer.

Nymphaea General Pershing is a new variety raised by George Pring at the Missouri Botanical Gardens as the result of a cross between N. Mrs. Whitaker and N. castaliaflora. The flowers are eight to ten inches across, opening from four to six days. They open early in the morning, usually about 7 a.m., and remain open until 7 p.m. The flowers are borne on stems twelve inches above the water and are very fragrant. The buds are dark green striped with dark purple; the sepals are light pink on the inside, and the petals a fine bright pink. A very free bloomer and a splendid addition to the pink day blooming varieties.

NYMPHAEA PULCHERRIMA
Tender Day Flowering

Nymphaea August Koch is a natural cross thought to be between N. Pennsylvania and Mrs. Woodrow Wilson. The seed from which the plant was raised was a pod of N. Pennsylvania, collected at Garfield Park, Chicago. The flowers average from seven to eight inches across on stems rising from eight to ten inches above the water. The sepals are purplish lilac, the petals pale wisteria violet. The leaves are peltate, averaging fourteen inches across, green on the upper surface. This Lily belongs to the daubeniana or viviparous class, young plants being produced at the surface of the leaves where the leaf and leaf stem meet. This is an excellent variety, very free in bloom and is highly recommended as a winter bloomer for the greenhouse tank.

Nymphaea capensis (Scutifolia) from Africa and Madagascar, produces flowers from six to eight inches across of a rich sky blue color. The sepals are green on the outside, white flushed blue on the face. The leaves are green, often tinted with purple, the underside frequently tinted red, brown spotted.

Nymphaea pulcherrima, a hybrid of Nymphaea coerulea, is a fine, strong growing plant, flowering very freely. The leaves are of large size, green, lobes long and tapering, the margin crenate; the underside green, thickly spotted with purplish brown. The flowers are from six to twelve inches across, light blue in color; stamens deep yellow tipped with blue; sepals striped and spotted black on the outside. The buds are long and sharp pointed, as in Nymphaea gracilis.

NYMPHAEA PENNSYLVANIA
Tender Day Flowering

In Nymphaea Pennsylvania we have the best of the light blue waterlilies. The flowers are of large size, from eight to twelve inches across, of a rich blue color; the stamens are yellow tipped blue; the sepals striped and spotted with purplish black. The leaves are green with dark brown spots. This plant is very free in growth and flower, several blooms being on the plant at one time. It flowers continuously from early in the season until frost.

Nymphaea ovalifolia from Africa was introduced by the U. S. Department of Agriculture. Flowers are medium to large, on long stems carried well above the foliage; of a creamy white color. The base of the petals is pale blue, deepening toward the tip to deep blue. A free flowering, sweet scented variety. This waterlily has proven to be an excellent one for the hybridizers.

NYMPHAEA GRACILIS
Tender Day Flowering

Nymphaea daubeniana has small, fragrant, light blue flowers; very free in flowering. This is an interesting variety as young plants develop at the junction of the leaf petiole and the leaf; these little plants grow, and when the leaf has reached full maturity and begins to decay, the little plant takes up its separate existence and flowers as freely and yields as large flowers as the parent.

Nymphaea Mrs. G. H. Pring. A new day blooming hybrid raised by G. H Pring, the result of a cross between N. ovalifolia and Mrs. Edwards Whitaker. This is a white flowered variety of great promise, the flowers averaging from eight to ten inches across, and of fine form. The petals are numerous, and of good substance. This is one of the best of the recent novelties.

NYMPHAEA MRS G. H. PRING

Nymphaea gracilis, from Mexico, gives beautiful star-shaped flowers, on strong stems, rising above the water from twelve to fifteen inches. The blooms are pure white., with deep yellow stamens, and are slightly fragrant. It flowers through the season very profusely, and is specially interesting as being the only white flowered day blooming tender waterlily with the exception of Mrs. G. H. Pring.

NYMPHAEA WM. STONE
(N. gracilis purpurea)
Tender Day Flowering

A number of seedlings have been raised from Nymphaea gracilis, with the Nymphaea zanzibariensis types as the other parent. The results of these crosses are a number of beautiful blue and pink varieties, all resembling Nymphaea gracilis in the form of flower, stem and habit of growth.

Nymphaea gracilis purpurea (Bisset) is identical with the last named, with the exception that the flower stems are light green.

Nymphaea gracilis purpurea (Sturtevant) has, on first opening, flowers of a rich purple color, fading to violet blue, stamens blue.

Nymphaea gracilis rosea perfecta (Sturtevant) produces flowers of large size, on stems well above the water, of a fine deep pink color, with very little of the purple generally found in Nymphaea zanzibariensis rosea, one of its parents. The flowers measure from eight to ten inches across.

Nymphaea gracilis rubra (Sturtevant) gives flowers from eight to ten inches across, of a deep rosy crimson color; stamens crimson; very much deeper in color than those of Nymphaea zanzibariensis rosea.

Nymphaea Wm. Stone produces flowers from six to eight inches across, of a violet blue color, stamens purple with a deep yellow center; sepals green on the outside, grayish blue on the inside.

They are carried on strong stems twelve to fifteen inches above the water. The flower stems of this waterlily are brown.

Nymphaea Mrs. C. W. Ward gives flowers of a deep rosy pink color, with golden yellow stamens tipped with pink. The flowers are from eight to ten inches across. This is a fine strong growing plant, as free in growth and flower as its parent, Nymphaea gracilis, and is a very desirable variety.

As Nymphaea mexicana is not hardy in the colder sections of the country it may be well to give a short description of it. The flowers are bright canary yellow, from four to five inches in diameter, rising on stems four to six inches above the water; the stamens are golden yellow, the leaves dark green blotched with brown; the underside dark crimson brown.

A selection of the best kinds would include the following: Nymphaea gigantea, Nymphaea Mrs. Edwards Whitaker, Nymphaea zanzibariensis, Nymphaea zanzibariensis rosea, Nymphaea Pennsylvania, Nymphaea General Pershing, Nymphaea gracilis, Nymphaea Mrs. Woodrow Wilson, Nymphaea Mrs. C. W. Ward, and Panama-Pacific.

NIGHT FLOWERING

The flowers of the night blooming waterlilies open as the evening falls, and remain open all night, commencing to close the following morning, if the sun is bright and clear, about 10 a.m. If the sky is overcast and the weather cool they remain open until 1 p.m. The time of closing of the flowers varies and is regulated very much by the weather, whether bright and warm, or cloudy and cool. Toward the end of the season, when the weather and water are cool, the flowers remain open day and night.

NYMPHAEA DENTATA SUPERBA
A beautiful night flowering white waterlily

Nymphaea lotus, of Egypt and Africa, is the sacred or white Lotus of the Nile. The leaves are dark green, from twelve to twenty inches in diameter. The flowers are white, from six to ten inches across, with broad concave petals often tinted pink.

NYMPHAEA DENTATA MAGNIFICA—A Hybrid
Tender Night Flowering

Nymphaea dentata, from Sierra Leone, gives very large, pure white flowers, measuring from eight to fifteen inches across; the outer row of stamens is pure yellow, the inner ones yellow with brownish purple spots near the base. The leaves are dark green, deeply dentate, from twelve to eighteen inches across. The plant flowers freely and continuously throughout the season. This is thought by many to be a variety of Nymphaea lotus, but the two are very different in flower, leaf and habit.

NYMPHAEA JUBILEE
Tender Night Flowering

Nymphaea dentata superba is a very fine waterlily, first offered for sale in the spring of 1906. It has a beautiful pure white flower, measuring from eight to twelve inches in diameter, with yellow stamens without any trace of purplish brown, making it the only one of this type that does not show the brown near the base of the stamens. The sepals are green, with faint, greenish white stripes on the outside, the inner side being white. This plant is also unique in that it comes true from seed. The leaves are large, deep glossy green, finely dentate. The plant flowers very freely.

Nymphaca dentata magnifica (a seedling from Nymphaea dentata X Nymphaea bisseti) (Bisset) is another white waterlily of the first rank. The flowers measure from eight to fourteen inches in diameter, have very wide petals, slightly concave, giving the flower a cup-shape that enhances its value. The stamens are pure yellow with purplish brown spots near the base. The leaves are heavily dentate with wavy crumpled margins; when exposed to the full sun the center of the leaf will take on a bronze color; they measure from twelve to eighteen inches in diameter.

NYMPHAEA DEVONIENSIS
Tender Night Flowering

Nymphaea Jubilee gives white flowers from six to eight inches across. The petals and sepals have a slight tint of pink at their base. The leaves are green blotched with brown on the underside; the margin is crumpled and wavy, deeply dentate.

Nymphaea devoniensis has the distinction of being the first hybrid among the beautiful night blooming waterlilies. It was raised at Chatsworth, England, in 1851, and named in honor of the Duke of Devonshire.

The flowers are from eight to twelve inches across, of a bright rosy red color, and are borne on fine, stiff stems well above the water. The stamens are cinnabar red. The surface of the leaves is dark bronzy green, greenish brown underneath. The leaves measure from twelve to eighteen inches in diameter. The plant blooms very freely, several flowers in all stages of development being in evidence at one and the same time.

Nymphaea rubra is very similar to the last mentioned. The petals are less pointed than in Nymphaea devoniensis, while the sepals are wider at the base. The leaves are mottled purplish brown on the underside, reddish bronzy brown on the surface, from twelve to eighteen inches in diameter. The flowers measure from six to ten inches across. There is little doubt that the true Nymphaea rubra has been lost to cultivation, and that what is here described as rubra is only a garden variety.

Nymphaea rubra rosea is a fine waterlily, producing blooms from six to ten inches across, of a deep brilliant, rosy carmine color. The petals are wide at the base, tapering to the point; the stamens are reddish brown at the tips and orange brown at the base. The leaves are deep green above faintly spotted brown with a slightly dentate margin.

NYMPHAEA RUBRA ROSEA
Tender Night Flowering

Nymphaea omarana (Bisset) gives flowers from eight to twelve inches across, of a beautiful rosy red shade with a faint tinge of white down, the center of the petals. The stamens are deep

NYMPHAEA OMARANA
Tender Night Flowering

orange red; the leaves deep bronzy green above, with dentate margin; the reverse brownish green. This is one of the finest and freest flowering of all the night blooming class and was named in honor of that well known horticulturist, the late Patrick O'Mara.

NYMPHAEA BISSETI
Tender Night Flowering

Nymphaea George Huster is a seedling from Nymphaea omarana. The color of the flower resembles that of Nymphaea rubra rosea, which was no doubt the pollen parent of this fine variety. The plant is as free in growth and flower as Nymphaea omarana, which it resembles in everything but the color of the bloom, which is a brilliant crimson.

NYMPHAEA STURTEVANTI
Tender Night Flowering

Nymphaea deaniana produces light pink flowers. The sepals are deep rose pink, both sepals and petals being very wide. The stamens are of a deep orange red color. The leaves measure from twelve to eighteen inches in diameter and are dark bronzy green.The flower is cup-shaped, after the style of that of its parent Nymphaea lotus, of which it is a seedling.

Nymphaea sturtevanti is a fine flower where it can be grown in a temperature of 80 degrees or over. It delights in heat, and is never at its best unless kept warm. The flowers, from eight to twelve inches across, are of a beautiful rosy pink; the petals very broad and incurving, giving the bloom a fine cup-shape. The stamens are orange brown in color. The leaves are large, bronzy green; the margins crumpled and wavy, with dentate edge.

The late E. D. Sturtevant, one of the pioneers in water gardening, standing by some of the plants he loved so dearly. Photograph taken in his California garden

Nymphaea Frank Trelease is the deepest colored of its class, the flower being a brilliant glowing dark crimson, measuring from eight to ten inches across. The stamens are deep reddish brown. The leaves are extra large, from fifteen to eighteen inches across, of a beautiful dark bronze color; the under side is greenish brown. This variety is similar to Nymphaea devoniensis in the form of the flower, but not so free in blooming, in which quality it is rather shy.

Nymphaea bisseti (Bisset) is another pink flower, of beautiful form, the result of a cross between Nymphaea dentata and Nymphaea sturtevanti. The flowers measure from eight to ten inches across, are of a beautiful rose pink color, the petals being extra wide, slightly concave, forming a cup-shaped bloom. The stamens are deep orange colored; the leaves deep bronzy green above, the underside brownish green with dark brown spots. The plant is very free in flower and growth.

Chapter X

VICTORIA REGIA

Flower of
EURYALE FEROX
First cousin to Victoria
regia

THIS remarkable waterlily was named in honor of the late Queen Victoria, by Dr. Lindley, who described and so named it, in 1837. It has very large, round, floating leaves from four to seven feet in diameter. The edges of the leaves are turned up from two to eight inches at right angles to the surface of the water, giving the leaf a platter-like appearance, hence one of its common names, "The Water Platter." Another popular name given it by the natives of South America is "Water Maize," or "Water Corn;" this is a very appropriate appellation as the seeds are gathered and eaten by these natives. The flowers, measuring from eight to fifteen inches across, open at dusk and remain open all night, partly closing about 10.30 a.m., and again opening at nightfall. The color of the flower when first expanding is a pure creamy white gradually changing, as the flower grows older, to pink, and then to deep purplish red on the second night. The flower is very fragrant, exhaling a sweet pineapple odor that is perceptible a great distance from the plant. The upper side of the leaf is of a rich green color; the lower surface of a deep purplish green, with many very prominent veins that radiate from the center to the margin of the leaf; these again are connected by smaller veins running transversely, so that the whole undersurface is divided into a number of irregularly arranged quadrangular compartments or pockets. The vein and leaf stalk are covered with strong spines. The underside of the leaf is well shown in the illustration.

The Victoria is represented by three well defined sorts which are native of South America, from British Guiana to Argentina. It was first discovered by Haenke in Bolivia in 1801; again by Bonpland near Corrientes, Argentina, in 1819, and by Poeppig, in 1832, on the Amazon River, who described it under the name of Euryale amazonica. D'Orbigny found it in 1827, at Corrientes, and again in 1833 in Bolivia, but he did not publish his record until a few years later. In 1836

Robert H. Schomburgk discovered the Victoria growing in the Berbice River in British Guiana, whence he sent specimens to England which Dr. Lindley described and named Victoria regia in 1837. Schomburgk, in describing the largest plant he saw, said that one leaf measured six feet five inches in diameter with a rim five to six inches high; the flowers were fifteen inches across. It may be of interest to state that the size of the leaf as here given has been exceeded in cultivation. On a plant grown in the Bartholdi fountain basin, in the United States Botanic Garden at Washington, D. C, in 1891, the largest leaf measured seven feet six inches across; the plant covered a space of forty-seven feet in diameter. This plant was grown without artificial heat after it was set out on the first of June; it was under the care of George W. Oliver.

A FINE PLANT OF VICTORIA REGIA, GROWN WITHOUT ARTIFICIAL HEAT, AT WASHINGTON, D. C.

The other species found at Corrientes was named Victoria cruziana, in honor of General Santa Cruz of Bolivia, by D'Orbigny, in 1840. This is the species that was introduced to American gardens in 1894, and the following year sent out as Victoria trickeri. It succeeds well in a much lower temperature than either Victoria regia or Victoria randi; therefore, is better adapted to outdoor culture. The plant is similar to Victoria regia in leaf and flower, except that the turned up edge of the leaf begins to show at a much earlier stage of growth. The leaf is also of a lighter green color all over the surface, with purplish green below while its upper edge is more even and uniform than in the other species in which it is rather uneven and ragged. This Victoria also flowers much earlier than either regia or randi, and requires less heat to bring it to perfection. The seeds will germinate in a temperature of 70 to 75 degrees and the plant can be grown in a temperature 10 degrees colder than can Victoria regia.

WELL GROWN SPECIMENS OF THE VICTORIA REGIA.

In 1840 Bridges obtained seeds of Victoria regia from the province of Moxos, in Bolivia, and sent them to Kew Botanical Gardens, England; from this seed three plants were grown but they died the following winter. Early in 1849, seeds arrived in England from two physicians named Rodie and Luckie, who sent them from the Essequibo River, in bottles of water. From these plants were raised, and on November 8 of the same year one flowered at Chatsworth, England. From this plant seed was distributed throughout Europe, some of it being also sent to America. The first plant grown in the Unted States was in the garden of Caleb Cope, at Philadelphia, Professor Thomas Meehan being the gardener. The first flower opened on August 21, 1851.

In 1886, the late E. D. Sturtevant, then of Bordentown, N. J., flowered a plant raised from seed that he obtained from Edward S. Rand, Jr., of Para, Brazil. This was quite distinct from Victoria regia, the flower being white, changing rapidly to deep crimson. The foliage was reddish colored, with very prominent reddish veins on the outside of the turned up edge of the leaf, the rim of which was deeper than in Victoria regia. This variety was named Victoria randi.

The Victorias require a high temperature and full exposure to sunlight to bring them to perfection, which cannot be done in the northern section of America without artificial heat. The plants will grow and do well in Washington, D. C., without artificial heat during the summer; but, ordinarily, they will not flower in time to ripen seed, rarely blooming until the letter part of August. The proper temperature for Victorias regia and randi is 85 to 90 degrees; Victoria cruziana will succeed in a temperature of 70 to 75 degrees.

FLOWER OF VICTORIA REGIA

The Victoria, as grown in gardens, is treated as an annual, the seeds being sown every year. These should never be allowed to become dry as this is fatal to them. As soon as they are gathered they should be kept in bottles of water. The seed should be sown in January or February, in a temperature as near to 85 degrees as possible for regia and randi, while those of cruziana should be sown in a temperature of 70 to 75 degrees. Before sowings file or cut a small hole through the hard outer shell of the seed, as is commonly done with canna seed. This method was first tried by James C. Clark, of Riverton, N. J., with wonderful success, in germinating the seeds of Victoria. Sow the seeds in a shallow fern pan, or pot, filled with fine soil without manure, and stand the pan in a tank of water, within four inches of the surface, placing it where it can have the full sunlight. If a heated brick or cement tank in which to start the seed is not available, a tank made of copper or galvanized iron should be procured, and the heat supplied by a small oil stove. By this means plants can be grown; but it is a very unsatisfactory method as the lamp will require very careful watching, and with the best of care the temperature of the water will fluctuate considerably. The best plan is to have a cement or brick tank located in the greenhouse, near the boiler, whence a separate flow and return pipe should be run to the tank, and around it, under the water, so as to secure the necessary temperature. When heat is not required in the other greenhouses the valves on the heating pipes entering these houses can be closed, thus keeping the tank at the desired temperature for the Victorias without having to carry the heat through the other houses when it is not needed there.

A LEAF OF VICTORIA REGIA

VICTORIA REGIA RANDI

Some of the seeds will germinate in from two to three weeks, while others may take much longer. As soon as the young plants have made the second, or floating leaf, they should be potted singly into two and one-half or three-inch pots, using soil which has passed through a one-half-inch screen, with the addition of one-third manure. The plants can then be placed in a tank where a temperature of 85 to 90 degrees can be maintained. The young plants should never be allowed to become pot bound, but should be shifted on into larger pots as they require it; and within three months they should be in eight- or ten-inch pots or pans. It is preferable to use a pan as, being of less depth, a shallower tank is required for its accommodation. The plants should not be set out in their summer quarters out of doors until settled warm weather has arrived. It must be remembered that as the Victorias come from a tropical climate, a sudden check would prove fatal to them; therefore, before planting in their summer quarters the temperature of the water in the basin in which they are to be placed must be the same as that in which the plants had previously been growing. If the basin is heated, the Victorias can be planted in the open any time after the first of May in the latitude of Washington and Philadelphia; for New York about the second week, and for Boston toward the end of the same month. The dates here given refer to an ordinary season, but in setting out any tender plant one should not be guided by the date but by the condition of the weather. A safe rule would be to plant the Victorias, if in a heated basin, as soon as it is safe to plant out Coleus in the open ground.

FLOWER OF VICTORIA REGIA CRUZIANA

The size of the basin necessary in which to grow a plant of Victoria should not be less than thirty feet across, with a depth of three feet at the center where the box or receptacle for soil will be placed. This box should be eighteen inches deep and from eight to twelve feet square. It is not necessary that the basin should have a uniform depth of three feet, the bottom can slope from this depth to from one foot six inches to two feet at the edge, if so desired. Also, it will be unnecessary to have the box full eighteen inches in depth, as one of one foot will answer as well, provided it is made large enough to afford the plant the same quantity of soil. Some means of heating the basin, in places farther north than Washington, D. C., is necessary in order to obtain the best results and the reader is referred to a previous chapter on "Heating the Tropical Waterlily Basin."

In greenhouse establishments where very tender tropical plants are grown a little fire is carried in the boilers through the summer; in such places it would be well to locate the Victoria tank near the boiler house, so as to utilize the same boiler for heating the tank.

When Victoria plants are ordered from growers of waterlilies, they are generally shipped in the pans in which they have been growing. On their arrival the temperature of the water in the pond should be taken, and if found below 80 degrees, the plants should be placed in a greenhouse tank; or if such a tank is not available, then a half barrel or any other receptacle large enough to hold the plant should be placed in the greenhouse, where the water surrounding the plant can be kept at the desired temperature until the water in the pond can be made warm enough for the safe planting of the Victoria outside in its summer quarters.

The Euryale ferox was, until the discovery of the Victoria regia, the largest and handsomest of all the aquatic plants in cultivation as to size of leaves, which resemble the young leaves of the Victoria before the edges turn up. The leaves of the Euryale are round, deep green in color, with many little rounded eminences on the upper surface; the underside is of a rich purple color with the same prominent veins and spines as seen in Victoria. The size of the leaves is from two to three feet in diameter; the flowers are small, about two inches across, of a deep purple color. The plant is a native of India and is cultivated near Bengal for its seeds, which are gathered, baked and eaten by the natives. The plant is a hardy annual as far north as Philadelphia, coming up every year from seed self-sown the previous summer, plants from which in turn will ripen seed and self-sow in a similar manner.

Chapter XI

THE SMALL WATER GARDEN

Selections of the Best Waterlilies and Aquatic Plants for the Beginner

THE best waterlilies for growing in a half barrel, if two plants are to be grown in one receptacle, are Nymphaea pygmaea, white; Nymphaea pygmaea helvola, yellow; or in place of either of these, Nymphaea laydekeri rosea, pink.

A half hogshead will accommodate two plants of the hardy waterlilies, of moderate growth. The best red or wine colored one is Nymphaea gloriosa; the best white, Nymphaea marliacea albida; the best yellow, Nymphaea marliacea chromatella.

For growing in a small tank the best hardy lilies are the last mentioned three and the following: Nymphaea andreana, Nymphaea James Brydon, Nymphaea W. B. Shaw, Nymphaea robinsoni, Nymphaea laydekeri rosea, Nymphaea marliacea rosea and Nymphaea gladstoniana.

The tender day flowering lilies are more vigorous in growth than the latter and, therefore, require more room. Only one plant can be grown in a half barrel, while two will be sufficient for a half hogshead. The best pale blue is Nymphaea Pennsylvania; Nymphaea gracilis is the only white day bloomer, excepting the new variety, Mrs. G. H. Pring. The best pinks are Nymphaea Mrs. C. W. Ward and General Pershing; the best dark blue, Nymphaea zanzibariensis. Nymphaea zanzibariensis rosea is a fine pink variety; the color ranges from light to deep rose pink. Nymphaea August Koch is an attractive violet blue lily; Mrs. Woodrow Wilson lavender blue.

The night flowering waterlilies are too strong and robust to be grown successfully in either a half barrel or hogshead. The best of these for a small basin would be the following: Nymphaea bisseti, pink; Nymphaea omarana, pink. The best whites are Nymphaea dentata magnifica and Nymphaea superba; rosy carmine, Nymphaea rubra rosea; purplish red, Nymphaea devoniensis.

A fine arrangement for a small lawn, where it is not desired to construct a basin, is to procure several half barrels, placing one in the center, raised above the level of the grass, and filling it with Nelumbium speciosum, which is a light pink; or Nelumbium album grandiflorum, if a white is preferred; or Nelumbium pekinensis rubrum, if a deep pink is desired. Around this center tub can be placed others containing a selection of the waterlilies previously named. Soil can be filled in between the barrels and in this soil some of the following plants set out; Cyperus papyrus; Cyperus alternifolius; Thalia dealbata; Sagittaria montevidensis; and, running over the soil as a carpet, the Myriophyllum proserpinacoides. These plants should be kept well watered, as they are all semi-aquatic subjects, delighting in lots of water.

Among aquatic plants other than the Nymphaeas, suitable for growing in tubs, Limnocharis humboldti is one of the best. It grows quickly and flowers profusely all summer, bearing yellow, poppy-shaped blooms.

Limnanthemum indicum is a very pretty plant for a tub; it bears little white flowers beautifully fringed, and blooms very freely all summer. Limnanthemum nymphaeoides gives pretty little golden yellow flowers, and blooms profusely all the season. These two plants can be grown in the same tub if the lasf named is kept pinched back so that it will not overrun the former and smother it.

The Water-hyacinth, Eichhornia speciosa, is also well adapted for growing in a tub, which should be half filled with soil, the remaining space with water, and the plants placed in the tub. They will soon root in the soil and commence to flower, continuing in bloom all through the summer. They flower best in a partially shaded position, or where the sun will only reach them during the morning and afternoon hours.

Eichhornia azurea is also a fine plant for a tub; it is a stronger plant than E. speciosa, but flowers as profusely throughout the summer.

Chapter XII

MISCELLANEOUS AQUATIC PLANTS

UNDER this head are included all plants that grow entirely submerged—roots, stems, and leaves—also such plants as grow in water but send up stems and leaves above the surface. The former plants are mostly grown in ponds and tanks where fish culture is carried on, as they are useful in keeping the water supplied with oxygen and also give the fish excellent material to spawn on, the eggs adhering to the stems and leaves. They are also grown in aquaria for the same purpose. The others are cultivated for ornamental purposes, many of them having flowers or attractive foliage to recommend them.

Acorus calamus (Sweetflag) grows to a height of two to three feet, and has lance-shaped leaves.

In Acorus calamus variegatus the young leaves are striped with a deep yellow, which fades to a paler color as they get older.

Acorus gramineus grows to a height of from eight to twelve inches, forming a round, grassy tuft.

Acorus gramineus variegatus is a beautiful variegated plant; the leaves are narrow, grasslike and striped with white. All the Acorus grow in shallow water or in damp soil, and are propagated by division of the root in spring or fall.

Anacharis canadensis gigantea (Giant Waterweed) is the finest submerged water plant for the fish culturist, or for the aquarium. It is a rapid growing plant, with dark green linear leaves and brittle stems. It will grow floating on the water or planted in the soil; it is perfectly hardy and a little of it in the pond will be useful as it is an excellent thing for the goldfish to spawn on. *Care should be taken however, that it does not get beyond control or it will prove a nuisance.*

Aponogeton distachyum (Cape-pondweed) is a very interesing aquatic plant from the Cape of Good Hope. The white flowers are borne on forked spikes and are arranged in pairs. They are very fragrant, having the odor of the Hawthorn. The anthers are purple, the leaves oblong, lanceolate, floating on the surface of the water. This is a fine subject for naturalizing in ponds where it can be planted in water of a depth of two feet and where the water does not freeze over. In the Northern States it is best lifted and carried over the winter in the greenhouse tank where it will flower toward spring and continue blooming for a long period.

Azolla caroliniana is a small, floating moss-like plant, which increases rapidly by self-division. When this plant is exposed to direct sunlight the small leaves take on a reddish tinge. It is useful for the aquarium.

LEAF AND FLOWER OF APONOGETON DISTACHYUS
Cape-pondweed

Butomus umbellatus (Flowering-rush) is a very pretty aquatic with narrow, three-cornered leaves from two to three feet in length. The flowers, which are purplish pink are borne at the end of a long, round stem. This plant will grow in shallow water in the pond or planted in wet soil; it is also useful for the aquarium if planted in soil in a pot.

Brasenia peltata (Watershield) is a plant with oval, entire, floating leaves. The flowers are small and purple colored. It is an interesting plant for the pond or for the aquarium.

Cabomba caroliniana (Fanwort) is another useful plant for the aquarium, growing entirely submerged; it emits roots readily. The leaves are green, oblong-linear. The flowers are one-half inch wide, white with two yellow spots. The plant is hardy as far north as New Jersey.

Cabomba rosaefolia is similar to the preceding except in the color of the leaves, which are tinged with pink on the underside; it is also more tender than Cabomba caroliniana.

The Cabombas are only desirable for aquaria or fish ponds. They should be planted in soil, in small pots, which can be hidden from view by placing stones around them on the bottom of the aquarium.

CYPERUS PAPYRUS
The Egyptian Paper Plant

Callitriche verna (Water-starwort) is a fine submerged plant, with dark green leaves, which grow close together at the ends of the stems, forming a mass of green, star-like cluster son the surface of the water. It should be planted in soil and kept near the surface; if kept in deep water it will soon die.

Callitriche autumnalis is similar to the former, but never rises above the surface of the water; therefore it can be planted at the bottom of the aquarium.

Caltha palustris (the Marshmarigold) grows to a height of from one to two feet, and bears bright yellow flowers. It should be planted in shallow water or in wet soil. Propagation is effected by division of the roots in early spring or when the plant is through flowering.

Ceratophyllum demersum (Common Hornwort) is another useful plant for the aquarium. The ends of the young shoots should be used. It has narrow, bristle-like leaves growing around the stem in whorls; the individual leaves are divided three or four times into forks, making a very dense plant. It grows entirely submerged, and should be planted on the bottom of the aquarium. This is a native plant found wild in ponds and still water in all sections of the country.

Cyperus alternifolius is one of the finest plants for growing at the edge of the pond in shallow water, or in the aquarium. It is also an excellent house plant, thriving well in the dwelling when other plants die. It requires a deep, rich soil for its best development, and is quite at home with its roots in water, either outdoors or indoors. As it is a tender plant it must be wintered in the greenhouse or dwelling. The picture on page 73 is reproduced from a photograph of a plant growing at the edge of a waterlily pond. The Cyperus is propagated by division or by young plants that grow on the top of the leaves.

Cyperus papyrus is the Egyptian Paper Plant. It is a fine, graceful plant for the water garden. Planted in a box of soil, a few inches below the surface of the water, it will grow rapidly and make a very fine specimen before fall. It grows from ten to fifteen feet in height, with long stems, at the top of which is the moplike head of fine, grasslike leaves. This plant is tender and should be removed to the greenhouse at the approach of frost. It is propagated from seed, also by division, which should be done while the plant is in a vigorous growing condition, either in summer or spring.

Eichhornia speciosa—Eichhornia crassipes major—(Water-hyacinth) is a showy, interesting, floating plant, much used in ponds and tanks. It cost the United States Government thousands of dollars in an effort to exterminate this plant from the St. Johns River, Florida, where it grew so luxuriantly that it obstructed navigation. However, this will never happen in the Northern States, as there it is a tender plant, always killed by a few degrees of frost, and therefore can never prove a weed. The petioles are inflated, forming a sort of bladder arrangement that keeps the plant afloat. If the water is shallow the plants will take root in the soil, and grow and flower more, freely than if floating around in the water. The flowers are borne on a stem about one foot in height, six to eight flow-flowers in a loose spike. The flowers are pale blue with a large blotch of deep blue and a yellow spot on the upper lobe.

Eichhornia azurea, a variety of the Water-hyacinth without the inflated stems of the preceding, is a strong, vigorous plant with large flower spikes. The flowers are of a beautiful shade of lavender blue. This plant thrives best in rich soil in shallow water. It can be planted in soil in a box submerged a few inches below the surface of the water. It is a tender plant and must be wintered in the house.

EICHHORNIA SPECIOSA—E.
crassipes major
Water-hyacinth

Fontinalis antipyretica (Willow-moss) is a native plant well adapted for the aquarium, being a fine plant for supplying oxygen to the water. The leaves are small and dark green. It is an excellent hardy plant, growing attached to stones submerged in the water.

Hippuris vulgaris (Marestail) is a plant found wild in the ponds and pools of the Northern States. The young plants are useful for aquaria. It has straight stems on which the leaves are arranged in whorls of from eight to ten. It grows entirely submerged.

Hydrocharis morsus-ranae (European Frogbit) is a graceful, floating water plant for the aquarium or pond. It is hardy and easily grown. The leaves are kidney-shaped, beautifully veined on long stalks. The pure white flowers are three petaled. Its method of self-propagation is very interesting. When the plant begins to ripen small buds are formed at the end of the runners, which drop to the bottom of the pond where they remain dormant until the return of warm weather, at which time they rise to the surface and begin to grow. After the buds have dropped to the bottom of the pond the old plant dies.

Jussiaea longifolia is another attractive aquatic plant, growing from two to three feet in height, and bearing numerous axillary, beautiful, bright yellow flowers. It is well suited for the edge of the pond, planted in shallow water, or for growing in a tub. It is best treated as a tender annual, the seed being sown in fall or spring, in shallow water. The seeds are very small and should be sown in fine soil; when the young plants have made three or four leaves, or as soon as they can be properly handled, they should be potted off into small pots and shifted as they require it until the time to plant them out arrives. It is not necessary to grow them in water. After the young plants have been potted off they can be grown on a bench where they can be well supplied with moisture.

Lemna minor (Small Duckweed) is found floating on the surface of the water in nearly all natural ponds in America. They are very small plants with small, ovate, light green leaves or fronds, having one rootlet attached to each frond.

Lemna polyrhiza is a larger plant than the foregoing. The leaves are nearly round and about one-half inch across, of a dark green color above and purplish underneath. Each leaf has a number of rootlets attached to the underside.

Lemna trisulca (Ivy-leaved Duckweed) has leaves of a light green color, about one-half inch in length, elliptical and very thin and serrated near the end. The young leaves grow at right angles to the old ones; attached to each leaf is one rootlet.

Lemna gibba (Thick-leaved Duckweed) has nearly round, thick leaves, about one-third of an inch across, flat above and rounded underneath, of a bright green color, with one rootlet attached to each leaf.

Limnanthemum indicum (Water-snowflake) is a very pretty little plant with light green, heart-shaped leaves. Its flowers come in clusters at the junction of the leaf and the petiole. The flowers are white with yellow centers; the petals are completely covered with little white, hairy glands. It thrives in rich soil, in shallow water, and is an excellent plant for a tub or for the aquarium, blooming profusely all summer. It is a tender plant and will require to be taken into the house before frost sets in.

Limnanthemum lacunosum (Floatingheart) is a pretty native hardy plant, with heart-shaped, mottled leaves, about two inches across. The flowers are small and pure white. For best results it should be planted in soil in the pond at a depth of water of from eighteen inches to two feet.

Limnanthemum nymphoides (Villarsia nymphoides) is a pretty aquatic plant with floating leaves, like those of a Nymphaea, and golden yellow flowers about one inch in diameter. The leaves are from two to four inches across. This is one of the best of the small aquatic plants; it is liable, however, to become a weed if not kept within bounds. It has become naturalized at Washington, D. C, but will require protection farther north.

Limnanthemum trachyspermum (Fairy Waterlily) resembles a miniature waterlily, and has leaves from two to three inches wide. The flowers are pure white, borne close to the leaves on the leaf stem. This is a native plant found growing in ponds from New Jersey to Florida.

All the Limnanthemums are best kept within bounds by planting them in submerged boxes and not allowing them to extend beyond an allotted space. They all flower profusely and are very pretty.

Limnobium bosci—Limnobium spongia—(American Frogbit) has leaves from one to two feet in length, of a dark green color, heart-shaped, tinted with purple underneath, and purplish roots. This is an evergreen plant and, not being hardy in the Northern States, will require to be wintered in the house.

Limnocharis humboldti (The Waterpoppy) is a beautiful little yellow flowered aquatic plant. The thick floating leaves are broad, oval, of a deep green color. The flowers pale yellow, from two to two and one-half inches across, are borne on stems that rise well above the water. It should be planted in soil, in shallow water not over eight inches in depth, and where it will have the full sunlight. It is a tender plant and, therefore, must not be exposed to frost. It is an excellent subject for a tub or for the aquarium in either of which it will flower profusely through the season. See illustration.

Limnocharis emarginata (Limnocharis plumieri) is an erect growing aquatic plant reaching out of the water to a height of from one to two feet. The leaves are cordate, four to six inches long, of a light green color. The flowers are pale straw colored from one-half to three-quarters of an inch in diameter. It likes rich soil and should be planted in shallow water in the pond. It is also desirable for the aquarium. The plants are tender and should be wintered in the house.

Ludwigia mulertti is a tender plant much used for aquaria purposes. The leaves are bright bronzy green above, tinted with deep crimson on the underside; they are oblong lanceolate. The flowers are small, yellow colored.

LIMNOCHARIS HUMBOLDTI
The Waterpoppy

Ludwigia palustris (Water-purslane) is found growing in wet soil or in shallow running streams and in ponds all over this country. The leaves are long, oblong; the flowers are small and reddish colored. It is useful for the aquarium.

Myriophyllum proserpinacoides (Parrotfeather) is a favorite aquatic plant for the aquarium and for fountain basins. The leaves grow in whorls of four to five; the segments are from twenty to twenty-five. This is a beautiful plant, having light green, feathery leaves. It is a strong, rampant grower, perfectly hardy from New Jersey southward. If not kept within bounds it will prove a great pest in the warmer sections of the country, as it will overrun everything. It is an excellent plant for the aquarium, where it should be planted in a pot of soil, and the pot hidden by stones on the bottom of the vessel. It is also a beautiful plant for the basins of fountains. The long stems grow out over the edge and droop gracefully over the stone, forming a curtain of living green. Another use to which it can be put is to treat it in the same way as the Japanese Fernballs are treated, that is, by planting the roots in a ball of moss and keeping it wet.

Myriophyllum verticillatum has submerged leaves, in whorls of three to four; the divisions are very fine and slender; also useful for the aquaria.

Myriophyllum spicatum has submerged leaves in whorls of four to five, dissected into slender capillary divisions; the floral leaves are ovate, entire or serrate; the flower spike from one to three inches long.

Myriophyllum heterophyllum has submerged leaves in whorls of four and five, linear or lanceolate. The flower spike is from twelve to eighteen inches in length. All of the Myriophyllums are useful for aquaria or for fish ponds.

Nuphar advena (Common Spatterdock) has large leaves about a foot in length, cordate-ovate to cordate-oblong; they are thick, nearly always with an open basal sinus. The flowers are from two to three inches across and are cup-shaped, not opening flat, yellow colored, often tinged with purple. Both flowers and leaves rise above the water.

Nuphar polysepalum is a larger plant than N. advena, with yellow colored flowers from four to five inches across.

Nuphar rubrodiscum has smaller leaves than N. advena. The flowers are from one to one and one-half inches across, yellow with the stigmatic disk bright red to crimson. They are suitable for planting near the edge of the pond, where they will soon establish themselves. They are not of great decorative value except for the leaves that rise out of the water.

Orontium aquaticum is a handsome aquatic perennial plant, growing from twelve to eighteen inches in height. It flowers in summer, and has a narrow spadix densely covered with small yellow blossoms. It should be planted at the edge of the pond, or in wet boggy soil. It is perfectly hardy.

Ouvirandra fenestralis (Latticeleaf) is one of the most interesting of aquatic plants. The leaves are skeletonized, of dark olive green color, floating just under the surface of the water; they are from six to eighteen inches in length, and from two to four inches wide. The flowers are borne on two spikes that are joined at the base, and carried on a stem about twelve inches long, rising above the water from two to three inches; they are very small and are borne in great numbers arranged around the two spikes. This is a tender greenhouse plant from Madagascar. It thrives best in a tub of water placed in a shady part of the greenhouse, where it will be kept at an even temperature of seventy to seventy-five degrees. It should be potted in a good rich soil such as has been recommended for Nymphaeas. Propagation is by division of the plant and from seed. The plant is often covered with algae; if this should happen, a few tadpoles or water snails of the Planorbis type, especially the variety corneus, which prefers algae and confervae growths to more valuable plants, will soon clear the leaves.

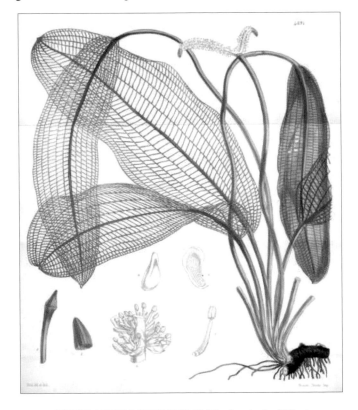

OUVIRANDRA FENESTRALIS—Latticeleaf Plant
View to the left shows the flower and a perfect leaf

Peltandra virginica (Water-arum) has dark green leaves, sagittate, on long petioles. The flower spathe is green, from four to eight inches in length.

Peltandra sagittaefolia (White Arrow-arum) has sagittate leaves, wider than those of P. virginica. The petioles are from eight to twenty inches long, the spathe whitish, from three to four inches in length; the spadix is much shorter than the spathe. The staminate flowers are borne on the upper half of the spadix.

The Peltandras are fine plants for shallow water, at the edge of the pond.

Pistia stratiotes (Waterlettuce) is a very ornamental aquatic plant. It forms a rosette of light green velvety leaves, with long, slender, feathery rootlets. The plant floats on the surface of the water and is from four to six inches across. It sends out side runners on which young plants develop. The Pistia likes a shady position and should be in water where its roots will reach the soil. Being a tender plant it must not be exposed to frost.

Potamogeton crispus (Curled-leaved Pondweed) is another useful plant for the aquarium. It has linear, oblong leaves, one-half to four inches in length and about one-half inch in width, slender, narrow and crimpled, serrated; the stems are long and flattened. This is a native plant found in ponds and slow-running streams; it likes a sandy soil.

Potamogeton natans has broader leaves than P. crispus. If planted in deep water the leaves will be long, grasslike, entirely submerged; other large, oval leaves will rise to the surface and float on the water. The flowers are small, green colored, borne on spikes above the water. It grows in ponds and slow-running streams and is principally used for aquarium purposes.

Proserpinaca palustris (Mermaidweed) grows to a height of twenty inches. The submerged leaves are oblong or linear lanceolate, one to two inches in length, very narrow and finely divided as in the Myriophyllum. It likes a sandy soil.

Proserpinaca pectinacea (Cut-leaved Mermaidweed) is similar to the preceding, but a smaller growing plant.

Pontederia cordata (Pickerelweed) is a fine, native aquatic plant found growing in shallow water. The leaves are arrow-shaped, carried on long stalks, rising from one to two feet above the water. The flowers are blue, borne on a close set spike. It is useful for planting in shallow water at the edge of the pond.

Ranunculus aquatilis (Watercrowfoot) is a fine plant for the aquarium. It is found in streams and ponds, sometimes covering the entire surface with its attractive leaves and flowers. The leaves are of two different types, the lower ones being always submerged and divided into numerous hairlike segments; the upper ones are three-lobed, with round notches, and float on the surface of the water. The flowers are white with yellow stamens.

Sagittaria montevidensis (Giant Arrowhead) is another fine plant for the edge of the pond in shallow water, or for planting in moist soil at the margin; it is also suitable for the aquarium. The leaves are arrow-shaped, with long, diverging basal lobes. The flowers are white with a purplish blotch at the base, and measure from two to three inches across. The plant will not stand frost and unless the roots can be planted below the frost line they should be taken up in the fall and stored in moist sand until the spring.

Sagittaria pusilla (S. natans) is a small growing plant with simple, slender, grasslike leaves, only growing a few inches in height. The flowers are white, one-half to three-quarters of an inch across, borne in a single whorl. The plant is only valuable for the aquarium. It can be planted in soil, or sand, at the bottom of the aquarium, and treated as a submerged subject. This is the small, grass-leaved plant so much used in aquaria.

DESIRABLE WATER PLANTS

Sagittaria latifolia is a very variable plant, growing from a few inches up to four feet in height. The leaves are broad sagittate, with long, basal lobes. The flowers are pure white, about one inch in diameter. It grows luxuriantly at the margin of ponds and streams, and is also useful for the aquarium.

Sagittaria sagittaefolia has a thick tuberous rhizome, the leaves are broad, sagittate. The flowers are white.

Sagittaria sagittaefolia flora plena (S. japonica fl. pl.) is very similar to the preceding, except that the plant bears large spikes of-pure white double flowers. This is a very desirable subject for the edge of the pond.

Sagittaria sinensis is a plant of similar habit of growth and leaf to S. pusilla, but larger in every way, growing more freely—a splendid plant for aquaria.

Salvinia braziliensis is a pretty floating aquatic plant suitable for the aquarium. It has slender stems with two-ranked oblong leaves, which are soft and green, covered with delicate hairs on the surface. This little plant should be taken into the house in winter. It is an annual and frequently dies in winter. After ripening its spores the spore capsules fall to the bottom and lie there until germination sets in. This, and S. natans, are supposed to be identical.

Saururus cernuus (Lizardtail) is a fine plant for the margin of the pond, reaching from two to two and one-half feet in height. It is a hardy perennial plant growing in swampy soil. The leaves are heart-shaped, and it has small, fragrant white flowers, borne on a dense terminal spike that curves gracefully over at the end. It flowers in June and July.

Scirpus lacustris zebrina (S. tabernaemontana zebrina) is a fine ornamental rush, growing from three to four feet in height, having beautifully variegated leaves with alternate bands of green and yellowish white. It grows well in shallow water, or when planted in a moist place. It is quite hardy.

Scirpus holoschoenus variegatus is the variegated form of the Siberian Rush. The stems are from twelve to eighteen inches in height, variegated with alternate bands of green and yellowish white. This plant grows in moist or ordinary garden soil. It also is hardy.

Stratiotes aloides has long, narrow, pointed, serrated leaves and large white flowers, borne on the end of stalks about six inches in length. It delights to root in the muddy soil at the bottom of the pond, where it remains entirely submerged, only coming to the surface of the water to flower. This is a fine aquarium subject and can be planted in the sand or allowed to float on the surface of the water.

Trapa natans (Waterchestnut) is a floating aquatic plant. The petioles of the floating leaves are from two to four inches long. The leaves themselves are about one inch in length, mottled or variegated. The flowers are reddish white. The seeds are large and black and are armed with four spikes or spines; they are edible and taste somewhat like chestnuts, hence the common name, "Waterchestnut." This plant likes to root in a good, rich, loamy soil. It is an excellent subject for the tub, aquarium or pond.

Trapa bispinosa has floating leaves of from two to three inches in length, the upper half slightly crenate; the petioles are from four to six inches long. The seed is about an inch long, broad and hairy, quite frequently with only two spines, or with the other pair just showing.

Typha latifolia (Cattail) is a fine hardy subject for planting at the edge of the pond in water or in wet soil. It grows in tufts of two-rowed flat leaves, eighteen to twenty-four inches long; the leaves from one to one and one-half inches wide. From the center of the leaves springs the flowering spike to a height of from six to seven feet. The flower is a close, cylindrical spike, six to nine inches in length and about one inch in diameter, of dark brownish black color.

Typha angustifolia is similar to the preceding except that the leaves and flower spike are narrower and more graceful.

Typha minor is a miniature form of T. latifolia.

Typha minima is a dwarf, growing only to a height of from twelve to eighteen inches, with dense, globose heads.

All the Typhas are excellent for shallow water treatment; they are perfectly hardy and are very attractive when in flower, with their black spikes and dark green, lance-like leaves.

Utricularia vulgaris is a hardy, native aquatic plant, with two to three pinnately-divided floating leaves, one-half inch in length, with fine, hairlike segments provided with bladders of a purplish color. The flowers are yellow, one-half to one inch long, on racemes of six or seven flowers on the upper end of the stalk, rising out of the water. This is an interesting plant for the aquarium.

Valisneria spiralis gigantea (Giant Eelgrass) is a hardy, submerged aquatic plant, with ribbon-like leaves, about half an inch in width and from one to two feet in length. The white flowers are borne on long, spiral, threadlike stems, rising to the surface of the water. This is a very useful plant for the fish pond and for the aquarium.

Vallisneria spiralis is similar to the last named but of smaller growth.

Zizania aquatica (Wildrice) is a fine plant for the pond, where it should be planted near the edge, in shallow water. The large, loose flower panicle is produced on stems of from five to ten feet in length. The plant forms a fine, grasslike clump, and is quite attractive. This is an annual and requires to be raised from seed every year; however, it will self-sow and come up annually.

Utricularia vulgaris

Chapter XIII

THE AQUATIC PLANT GREENHOUSE

FOR best results in the cultivation of tropical waterlilies a heated tank in the greenhouse is necessary; here the plants can be started into growth early in the year, so as to have them in six or eight inch pots when planting out time comes. Plants from this size pot will commence to bloom at once and, therefore, give a longer flowering season than if smaller plants are set out. Any style of greenhouse will answer for this purpose. The ideal structure, however, is an even span house, about twenty feet wide inside measurement, with brick or concrete walls; a tank on either side three feet wide, with two walks, each two feet six inches wide, and a tank down the center six feet four inches wide. This will allow of four side walls eight inches thick for the tanks.

It is well in building tanks for the growing of waterlilies in the greenhouse to have them of a width so that all the plants can be reached from one side or the other. The center tank should be equally divided by a partition, so that one-half can be kept warmer than the other. One tank should have a two-inch heating pipe run around the sides (for number of square feet of pipe required see pages 11 and 47); each of them should be supplied with a valve so as to enable the operator to control the temperature of the water. Most of the time one pipe will be sufficient to maintain the necessary temperature. The cooler tank should have one two-inch pipe down the center, valved so that the heat can be regulated. The greenhouse should be piped to maintain a temperature of 70 degrees in the coldest weather.

If the system of overhead heating is carried out, the pipe entering the tanks can be dropped from the flow pipe, run to the far end of the tank and there connected with the return to the boiler. Where the pipes go through the walls of the tank, it is advisable to have a large pipe, of the same length as the wall is thick, built into the wall for the heating pipes to pass through. This will prevent the cracking of the wall by the expansion of the heating pipe. The wall can be made tight where the pipe goes through, by using the long screw and washer described on page 46.

It is needless to say that all pipes and fittings used in the tanks should be galvanized to prevent their rusting. The tanks on the sides of the house need not be over twelve inches deep. For the center tank a depth of eighteen inches will be found very satisfactory. One of the side tanks should have heating pipes around it so as to insure a temperature of 80 degrees. About four feet of this tank should be partitioned off at one end, and extra pipes run in so as to carry a temperature of 85 to 90 degrees. In this tank the Victoria regia can be grown. The other side tank need have no heating pipes and could be used principally for carrying over stock. All the tanks should be provided with an overflow and an outlet. One pipe can be made to answer for both of these by having a piece of pipe, with an L-shaped pipe screwed on to it, built into the bottom of the tank so that the mouth of the L-shaped pipe will turn upward; into this L-shaped pipe a piece of pipe can be loosely screwed of sufficient length to reach the water level in the tank, which should be about one inch below the top of the wall. When it is desired to empty the tank the standpipe may be easily unscrewed and the water thus allowed to escape.

Aquatic plant greenhouse

Another house, less pretentious, nevertheless very satisfactory, is to have a tank located outside of sufficient width to be covered by hotbed sash. The walls of this tank can be formed of concrete or brick and the back wall carried up eighteen inches above the front one so as to shed the rain. The side walls should slope with the pitch of the roof. A boiler pit can be dug at one end and a small boiler installed to heat the tank. The flow pipe rounding growth. No plant should be used, however, that will not stand full exposure to direct sunlight in which the waterlilies delight, so the glass should never be shaded. The ground around these plants can be covered with Tradescantia or other low creeping subjects, and at the edge of the tanks can be grown Limnocharis humboldti, Limnanthemum indicum (Water-snowflake), Eichhornia crassipes major, Eichhornia azurea, etc. The plants named, with the exception of the Snowflake, are rather strong and vigorous and will have to be kept in place or they will soon cover the water.

Aquatic plant greenhouse

The tanks can be built either of brick or concrete. The smaller ones should have a depth of two feet; the larger one, where the Victoria regia is to be grown, should be three feet deep. The walls of the tank should be finished with a suitable coping and extend about twelve inches above the ground level.

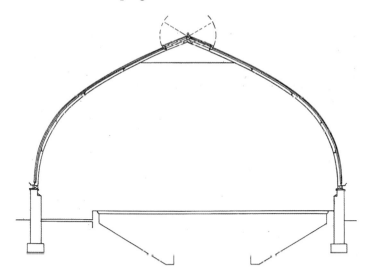

CURVILINEAR GREENHOUSE FOR AQUATIC PLANTS

Waterlilies for Winter Flowering

Waterlilies are frequently grown for their flowers in the greenhouse during winter. They afford a change from the ordinary florist's stock, and are always acceptable to the flower lover. The varieties that give good satisfaction during winter are the day flowering blue lilies, Nymphaea Panama-Pacific, N. Pennsylvania, N. Mrs. Woodrow Wilson, N. August Koch. These will often have four or five flowers open at one time. The night flowering Nymphaeas dentata superba and dentata magnifica will give fine white flowers. Nymphaea omarana and Nym-phaea bisseti are beautiful pinks that bloom very freely throughout the winter months. For a very deep red, none will prove more desirable than Nymphaea rubra rosea.

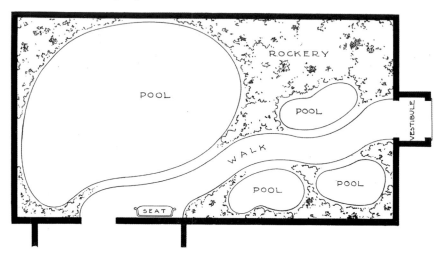

Courtesy Lord & Burnham Company, New York
INTERIOR PLAN OF AQUATIC CURVILINEAR GREENHOUSE

Young plants of the varieties named should be potted up during August, and kept growing by giving them larger pots or boxes as required. On the approach of cold weather the plants should be removed to the greenhouse tank, where a temperature of 75 to 80 degrees can be maintained in the water. The plants will commence to flower immediately and continue blooming throughout the winter.

Aquatic plants grown in a greenhouse

A greenhouse, with tanks as described on preceding pages, will prove an ideal structure for the growth of waterlilies for winter flowers. No special cultural directions are required for the greenhouse treatment of waterlilies; simply have the plants well established before cold weather arrives. The plants will make more growth in one day in August than in several days in November, hence the directions to commence work in the former month. The water in the tanks should be kept as near to the temperature mentioned as possible. See that all decaying leaves are removed, and the plants syringed with a good force of water daily; this will hold the black aphis in check, as well as keep the plants clean.

While a large number of flowers will be cut from a plant during winter, the plants do not bloom free enough, for the amount of space required for their proper cultivation, to induce anyone to erect greenhouses for their cultivation exclusively, with the intention of selling the flowers.

Chapter XIV

PROPAGATION OF WATERLILIES

Raising Waterlilies from Seed

SEEDS for waterlily propagation require a tank or other vessel that will hold water, and some means of heating the same, unless the seed can be placed in a warm greenhouse, when the temperature will keep the water sufficiently warm. The seed should be sown and the pots (or pans) kept submerged in water at a temperature of from 70 to 80 degrees. Sow the seed as soon after January first as possible, in pots, pans or boxes. The most useful and easily handled, taking very little water to cover it, so that it can be placed in a very shallow tank, is the shallow Fern pan so often used for jardinieres for table use. This should be filled to within one inch of the brim with very finely screened soil, as described in a previous chapter. Sow the seed and place over it a light covering of sand that has first been put through a fine screen. The pan should then be lowered into a vessel of water, about four-fifths submerged, and allowed to remain there for a day. The water will be absorbed by the soil, and the seed thoroughly soaked. If the pan should be immersed at once after sowing, the seed, being dry, will float on the surface of the water and, if several varieties are sown at the same time, become mixed. By following the method described none of the seed will float if it be in good condition.

After the pans have been in the water long enough for the seed to become thoroughly soaked they should be placed in the tank, allowing an inch or two of water above the soil. It makes very little difference how deep the pans are submerged, as the seeds will grow if sown eighteen inches under water, and will send their leaves to the surface in due time.

The pans containing the seed should be placed at one end of the tank, which should be divided off from the remainder by a partition of fine wire to protect the seed from the goldfish, as these, if allowed free play, will very soon scatter both seed and labels over the tank. If it is not practicable to divide the tank, then a small piece of one-quarter inch mesh wire should be cut to fit over each pan. It is absolutely necessary to have the seed protected in some way when goldfish are in the same tank with it.

Lotus seed pod

When the seedlings first make their appearance they look very much like fine grass. They should not be transplanted until they have made what is termed the first floating leaf; that is, the first leaf to rise to the surface and float on the water. They should be potted singly into two-inch pots, or transplanted into boxes, two inches apart each way. The boxes should be two inches in depth, and of any size that can be easily handled. A box fifteen by eighteen inches is a very convenient size. The soil should have incorporated in it a little well decayed manure, and should not be too coarse. After potting, or boxing, the soil should be covered with a layer of fine gravel that has been passed through a screen of one-half inch mesh. If gravel cannot be obtained coarse sand will answer. This will keep the goldfish from digging in the soil, and prevent them setting afloat the young plants. Nothing better than gravel can be employed for this purpose, and it should be used always on pots and boxes, both in the greenhouse tank and in the larger boxes in the pond. After the young plants have filled the two-inch pots with roots, or begin to crowd each other in the boxes, they should be afforded larger pots, using soil a little coarser than at first, and with more manure in it. When the plants reach the three-inch pot stage, they can be potted in the soil recommended for the larger plants.

The plants should be repotted whenever they have filled the pots with roots, in the same way as a Geranium or Rose would be treated. The aim should be to keep the young plants in a good growing, healthy condition, and this can only be done when they have sufficient root room and plenty of good soil. Therefore, see that the young plants have all that they want to keep them growing vigorously until the time arrives for planting them out in their summer quarters.

Waterlilies that are easily raised from seed, and that are sure to give satisfaction, are those of the zanzibariensis section. Nymphaea zanzibariensis is a fine dark purple lily that will not always come true from seed. The seedlings obtained from the true dark purple variety will give flowers ranging in color from deep blue to pale lavender. Nymphaea zanzibariensis azurea, as the name denotes, gives pale sky-blue flowers; it is grown extensively from seed. Nymphaea zanzibariensis rosea, a pink-flowering form, is also easily raised from seed. These three day bloomers are the best to commence with and, after being successful with them, the experiment can be tried of raising the more difficult ones.

In the night blooming class, Nymphaea dentata, a large pure white, is readily raised from seed. A fitting companion to this is the beautiful night blooming pink lily, Nymphaea omarana. Both of these can be raised from seed and, if sown early, the seedlings will flower the first year.

The seeds of the hardy lilies take longer to germinate, and are slower to reach maturity. Seeds of some of the tender lilies will germinate in ten days; but those of the hardy sorts often take three months and have been known to lie dormant for a year and then grow. The best results are obtained by sowing the seeds of the hardy lilies as soon as harvested in the summer. They can be sown in boxes or pans, and placed in the pond or tank out of doors, where they will germinate and make a few leaves. Before the water becomes too cold to chill the young plants, these receptacles should be removed to a cool greenhouse or a frost-proof cellar, and the plants kept covered with a few inches of water. They should not be disturbed until growth commences in spring. When the plants have made a few new leaves they can be transplanted into pots or boxes, which will keep them growing until the time to plant them in their summer quarters.

Seedlings of all of the tender night flowering and day flowering varieties can be raised in the same way. If the seed is sown as soon as ripe, through July and August, most of the young plants will form small tubers before frost, which will carry them safely through the winter in quarters similar to those recommended for the hardy sorts.

If neither greenhouse nor tank be available in which to raise the seedlings, one need not despair, for many fine plants of the zanzibariensis section have been grown in nothing better than an ordinary porcelain bowl. The truth is, seeds of waterlilies can be germinated in any vessel that will hold water kept sufficiently warm. A method that is very satisfactory, when one has no tank in which to sow the seed, is to fill a pot with fine soil, as recommended above, sowing the seed and then standing the pot in a saucer kept full of water. The soil will absorb the water by capillary attraction, and this will keep it sufficiently wet to germinate the seed and start the young plants growing for several weeks. When they begin to crowd each other they should be potted off singly, and the pots submerged in water. In sowing seed by this latter method care should be taken to have the soil sweet, and enough sand should be added to the soil so that the proportion will be one-half of each.

If it is not desired to raise the plants from seed, young plants in all stages of growth can be purchased from the dealers in this class of stock. In this way, fine healthy plants can be secured that will be sure to flower early in the season, as the growers are well equipped with heated tanks to raise these plants to perfection.

Propagation of Tender Waterlilies

To get tubers of the tender waterlilies for stock raising, a few plants of each variety should be grown in small pots all summer. The pots should not be larger than six or seven inches in diameter. The plants will soon exhaust the food in the soil and then will commence to form small tubers. When the plants have ripened up, which will be shown by the leaves becoming yellow, brown and red, the pots should be taken from the water and laid on their sides in a moist place under the greenhouse bench, where they will not dry out too rapidly, and where is maintained a temperature of from 50 to 60 degrees. Here they should remain, protected from mice and rats, until spring.

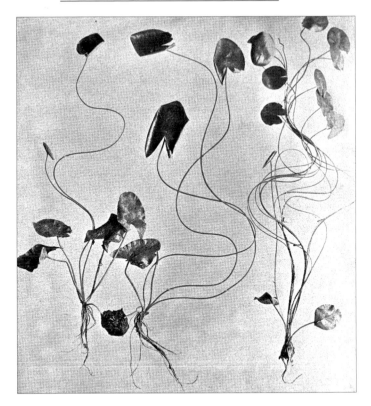

TYPES OF ROOTS OF THE WATERLILIES
To the left, a tuber of the night blooming section, showing two young
plants ready to be separated. To the right, a tuber of zanzibariensis type,
showing a small tuber with one young plant

Tender waterlilies are generally raised from the tuberous roots which are started into growth from the month of January on, according to the supply of stock. In the case of a new variety, of which the stock is limited, the tubers can be grown all winter and the young plants potted up as formed. The tubers are generally wintered under the greenhouse bench where they are placed when taken from the pond in the fall, in pots or boxes of sand kept moist but not wet. The tubers are placed in pots, in shallow pans or boxes, in a light soil that has been passed through a fine screen. This screening of the soil is to insure the safe removal of the fine white roots, when the young plants are separated from the tuber, which would surely be broken if coarse soil was used. After potting, they should be placed in a heated tank in the greenhouse, four or five inches below the surface of the water, which should be kept at a temperature of from 75 to 80 degrees. The tubers will soon commence to grow, sending out shoots the same as the potato does. These shoots then send out leaves and, at the base of the leaf stems, roots are emitted. As soon as the young plants have one or two floating leaves they should be separated from the parent tuber and potted singly into two and one-half or three-inch pots, using a little coarser soil with the addition of one-third rotted cow manure. After the young plants have been removed the tubers can be replaced in the boxes or pans, and will give another crop of young plants in a few weeks. After potting, the young plants the soil should be covered with a layer of coarse sand, or fine gravel, and the plants placed in a tank where the same temperature can be maintained as that in which they had been previously growing. The pots should be immersed deep enough to allow the floating leaves to reach the surface of the water. If they should be placed in deeper water than here stated, no harm will come to them, as, if strong and robust, they will send the leaves to the surface even if there is eighteen inches or two feet of water above the plants. All that is now required is to see that the young plants are kept in a growing condition, without any check from cold, or by becoming pot bound. They should be repotted into larger pots as required, using soil with one-third to one-half cow manure. As the size of the pot increases, the soil used can be coarser in texture until the ordinary compost soil is employed.

The zanzibariensis types make small conical tubers that should not be allowed to go to rest. The best method of handling this type, after lifting the plants from the pond, is to pot them up into as small pots as will contain them, wintering them in a rather cool tank where they will have a temperature of fifty-five to sixty degrees, in which temperature they will remain in a semi-dormant condition, ready to start into growth with the warmer weather of spring. They sometimes make side tubers which can be separated and potted up, or carried through as recommended above for the night flowering class.

TYPICAL ROOTS OF HARDY WATERLILIES
The illustration to the left showing a branching type with crowns close together. To the right is shown a long running root with a young shoot growing from the side. The white lines show points of separation for purposes of propagation.

The tubers of this class do not send out a number of shoots as do those of the dentata class, yielding but one single plant from the top of the tuber. This plant, when well rooted, can be removed and potted and the old tuber returned to the tank, when a month or two later it may give another young plant.

The tubers of the gracilis types can be kept dormant all winter, stored in sand, in the same manner as the night flowering types, and treated similarly to them. To this class belong Mrs. C. W. Ward, gracilis purpurea, William stone, and gracilis.

By Division

The hardy waterlilies are propagated by division of the rhizomes. Some of them bear seed and can be increased by this means, but to get them to come true to type it is necessary to divide the root.

Some of the lilies have long, thick spreading roots, with a large number of growing points, or eyes, on them; others have a single thick crown which cannot be divided. Laydekeri rosea is a good example of this class. Plants of it can only be procured from dealers in waterlilies.

Lilies of the odorata section have long spreading roots, with many growing points on each root; these can be cut off, a few inches in length, planted singly in boxes or pots, and within a short period will make flowering plants.

Nymphaea pygmaea is raised from seed and not by division.

The hardy lilies can be divided at any time the plants are in active growth. The best time to divide them, however, is in spring, just as active growth commences. The next best time is about August, as they will then have time to get well rooted in their new quarters before freezing weather.

Hybridizing and Seed Saving

The hybridizing of waterlilies is governed by the same principle as the hybridizing of other plants. The first thing to do is to select the parent plants. This should be done with care, having in mind what is desired in the progeny. To avoid disappointment make sure that the plant selected for the seed parent is a fertile and not a sterile one, so many of the finest of the waterlilies being sterile.

Having selected the seed bearing plant, an unopened flower bud should be chosen at least a day before its natural opening period, and the stamens removed. The flower should then be covered with a fine gauze, thus preventing pollen from other flowers being deposited on the stigma by flies or bees. A day earlier the pollen bearing plant should be selected., and a flower bud a little further developed, or nearer to opening, chosen and similarly-covered. The following morning, or the first day of the natural opening of the seed bearing flower, the pollen should be gathered. This is best done by cutting the flower, being careful not to wet it, holding it inverted over a paper, or glass, and giving it several sharp taps, thus precipitating the pollen onto the receptacle on which it is to be carried to the flower to be pollinated. Remove the gauze and, with a camel's hair brush, distribute the pollen evenly over the stigma. The gauze is then replaced and, within a week, if the cross has been successful, the seed pod will begin to swell; if unsuccessful, the pod and stem will commence to decay. As the seed vessel increases in size, an examination should be made to see that the gauze does not press too hard on the pod, otherwise the gauze may burst and the seed be lost.

A close watch should be kept on the seed vessel so that it does not burst unexpectedly and some of the seed be lost through the decaying of the stem at the junction of the pod. A sure sign that the pod is nearly ripe is that it will rise to the surface of the water a few days before it bursts; whenever it appears there it can be picked and placed in a pan of water, where it will complete the process of ripening and then burst. The seed should then be washed clean and dried or sown.

When seed that will produce plants true to type is desired, the flowers should be covered in the same way as for hybridizing, but without removing the stamens. Some of the waterlilies, especially the hybrids, will not bear seed; others that do bear it very rarely come true from seed. Therefore, it is always the surest method, when the true type is wanted, to purchase plants or tubers and not seed.

In sowing the seed, the pods, when first gathered, should be placed in a vessel of water to ripen and burst; these vessels should be of a size that can be easily handled when washing the seed. When the pod bursts the seed will float on the surface of the water. The seed has a fleshy covering, given to it by nature for its proper distribution, the seed being carried by the wind and currents all over the pond. In twenty-four hours most of the seeds will have fallen to the bottom of the vessel. They should then be thoroughly cleansed by being rubbed through the hands, washed several times in clean water and, if of the tender varieties, be spread out to dry. When dry they should be stored in bottles or other receptacles until it is time to sow them in spring.

Seed of the hardy varieties should be sown at once, or kept in a bottle of water at a low temperature, as they soon lose vitality if allowed to dry.

WATERLILIES THAT BEAR SEED

The following hardy waterlilies will bear seed: Nymphaea reniformis (Tuberosa), N. r. rosea, N. r. richardsoni, N. gladstoniana, N. mexicana, N. flava, N. odorata, N. o. caroliniana, N. o. gigantea, N. o. minor, N. o. rosea, N. o. W. B. Shaw, N. o. luciana, and N. pygmaea.

Tender Day Flowering: Nymphaea capensis, N. coerulea, N. gracilis, N. zanzibariensis, N. z. rosea, N. z. azurea, and N. elegans. Nymphaea Pennsylvania and N. pulcherrima frequently bear seed, but cannot be depended on.

Night Flowering: Nymphaea lotus, N. dentata, N. d. superba, N. d. magnifica, N. bisseti, N. omarana, N. George Huster, N. Jubilee, N. rubra rosea, and N. deaniana.

The author has succeeded in securing and ripening a seed pod from Nymphaea sturtevanti by crossing it with pollen from N. rubra rosea, although it is not a seed bearer under ordinary circumstances.

TYPES OF HARDY
WATERLILIES

Chapter XV

FOR THE COMMERCIAL CUT FLOWER GROWER

Suitable Ponds, Culture, and Varieties

WATERLILIES are now in great demand as cut flowers. In their season they are extensively employed for the decoration of florists' windows, and also in funeral designs. The tender night flowering lilies open their flowers about 7 o'clock, in time for the decoration of the dinner table, and for this purpose they are unsurpassed. The flowers are large, of beautiful colors that show up well under artificial light. A low vase of these flowers, with their leaves of light green ranging to deep bronzy red, hanging over the edge of it and almost touching the tablecloth, forms a beautiful decoration indeed. The hardy waterlilies are especially appropriate for the sick chamber, bringing with them, as they do, their exquisite colors and a sweet, delightful fragrance all their own.

For the successful cultivation of these plants commercially, suitable ponds are necessary. A location should be selected that is comparatively level, or low and swampy, and near a water supply, preferably some brook or stream, and the pond dug, the material excavated being thrown up on the sides to form walks that will be high and dry. The pond should be large, and if in low, wet ground will require no clay or concrete to make it watertight. A pipe for an overflow and draw off should be located at the end of the pond farthest from the inlet, where the water can run off by gravity. The size of this pipe will depend on the dimensions of the pond; but whatever the size of the pond, there will be nothing gained by using a small pipe, as when the pond is to be emptied the work should be done quickly and this can only be accomplished with a pipe of good size. For a pond of about one hundred by one hundred feet, a six-inch pipe will be sufficient; this size can be taken as a guide for larger ponds.

A pond of a depth of eighteen inches will be ample for the growth of all waterlilies and for the protection of the roots from frost in Winter. At this depth the caretaker can wade in with hip rubber boots to attend to the cultivation of the plants and to cut the flowers. In localities where ice forms below the depth mentioned the pond must be further excavated so that the roots of the waterlilies will not be frozen. Some of the plants will not be injured by the freezing of the roots; but others, and some of them the best, will be killed if allowed to freeze.

The pond excavated, the bottom should be laid out in beds of sufficient width and length to accommodate the number of plants of one variety it is desired to plant. To form these beds, boards of one inch thickness and twelve inches wide are sunk into the soil, on edge; these are kept in position by posts, thus forming a solid bed as it were. These boards prevent the roots from running through the pond and getting intermixed with others; this they would soon do, with but few exceptions. Between each bed a lane or walk, of from three to six feet, according to the growth of the plants, should be left. This lane, being clear of leaves, will allow a boat to get in and out among the waterlilies without damaging the plants when cutting the flowers, and to otherwise attend to their wants.

When the beds are ready, they should have a heavy dressing of from four to five inches of cow manure spread evenly over the surface, and dug in. The ground being low, good soil will be found below that which was taken out. The beds will then be ready to receive the plants, which can be set out from four to six feet apart, according to the growth of the variety. When planting is completed enough water should be turned into the pond to cover the roots to a depth of from two to three inches, and no more water added until the plants have commenced to grow. When the plants are sending out leaves more water can be added, and a few days afterward the pond can be entirely filled.

The tender waterlilies, with the exception of one or two, do not send out running shoots or rhizomes; therefore, it is not necessary to board up the beds where these are to be grown. All they require is that the manure be spread and dug in where they are to grow, and that they be planted from six to ten feet apart when the proper time comes, which is in May or June, according to latitude. Where tender waterlilies are grown in the same pond with the hardy ones, the beds for the former should be prepared at the same time as those for the latter; this will avoid drawing off the water when planting the tender ones, as they can be planted from a boat, or by wading into the pond. The tender waterlilies will have been grown in the greenhouse tank, and therefore will have leaves on long stems which will rise to the surface of the water; they also will be well established plants with plenty of roots, and will not be injured by being planted in deep water.

The Nelumbiums should have a pond to themselves, as they are strong, robust plants, with long roots that often run from fifteen to twenty feet in a season; on this account, unless the roots can be confined, they are unsuited for growth in a pond with other plants. They like a rich, deep, clay soil, to which has been added from four to six inches of cow manure, spread evenly over the soil and dug in. The best form of pond or tank for Nelumbiums is a long, narrow one, just wide enough to allow of the flowers being gathered from the walks on either side of the pond. This would give a width of from six to seven feet for the pond, and a walk of from three to four feet on each side, with every alternate walk wide enough to allow of the passage of a wagon with manure. The Nelumbiums do not require as much water above the soil as the waterlilies, for they root very deep in the mud, far below the frost line; therefore, a depth of twelve inches of water will be quite sufficient for them.

After the first preparation of the soil as described for both waterlilies and Nelumbiums, all that will be required in after years will be to afford a heavy coating of cow manure and a generous sprinkling of bonemeal, about one-half pound to the square yard, applied every spring, and dug in or trampled in with the feet around the plants.

The waterlilies selected to produce cut flowers for the commercial grower should have the following essential points: They should give good sized fragrant flowers, of good form and color; the plants should be strong and of robust, healthy growth, free and continuous in flower.

The following have been selected as approaching nearest to this standard of excellence; some are better than their fellows in a few particulars, while in others they fall behind. If the varieties named are planted, there will be an abundant supply of flowers throughout the season, of good size and color. Preference should be given to the varieties marked with an asterisk (*).

In white, *Nymphaea odorata gigantea, *Nymphaea gladstoniana, *Nymphaea alba candidissima, *Nymphaea marliacea albida, Nymphaea reniformis richardsoni.

Pink: *Nymphaea marliacea rosea, *Nymphaea odorata rosea, *Nym-phaea Wm. B. Shaw.

Pink to crimson shades: *Nymphaea gloriosa, *Nymphaea James Brydon, Nymphaea rubra punctata, *Nymphaea andreana, Nymphaea lucida.

Yellow: *Nymphaea marliacea chromatella.

Yellow, overlaid with purplish red: Nymphaea robinsoni.

Nelumbiums: Album grandiflorum is the best white; Nelumbium pekinensis rubrum is the best deep pink; Nelumbium pekinensis rubrum flore pleno the best double deep pink; Nelumbium Shiroman is a fine double white; Nelumbium speciosum is the beautiful delicate pink Lotus, commonly known as the Lotus of the Nile.

NYMPHAEA MARLIACEA ROSEA

Chapter XVI

TENDER SUBTROPICAL PLANTS FOR MARGINS AND BORDERS

THE environments of the waterlily pond must be made attractive, and to obtain this result it is in keeping to have the borders and beds surrounding it filled with subtropical plants; especially are these features appropriate if the large, tropical lilies are growing in the pond. If the pond has been protected from high winds, as recommended, the subtropical plants should do well in nearly all sections of America. The plants being well sheltered the leaves will not be rent in shreds during every windstorm, which is the great drawback to the cultivation of the Musa and other large-leaved plants in the open ground; otherwise, after each wind blow, they are left in a very unsightly condition and remain so until new leaves develop.

Following we give a brief descriptive list of the most interesting and best adapted plants for the beautifying of the margins of the pond:

Alocasia macrorhiza variegata has a green leaf mottled and blotched with white; the leaves are sometimes all white. This plant should be set out where it will be shaded from direct sunlight, and at the end of the season be potted up and kept growing all winter.

Another plant that should have a similar position is Calathea (Maranta) zebrina. It delights in a shady spot. The leaves are beautiful velvety green barred with purplish green; the underside is a deep violet purple. Planted out, the leaves will grow to a length of three feet and a width of twelve inches. This plant should be potted at the approach of frost and wintered in the greenhouse.

Cannas are always in good taste placed in the subtropical border, and especially those with large foliage. Canna ehmani, for this purpose, is one of the best; it has extra large green leaves, three feet long by eighteen inches wide, the plant growing to a height of ten feet; the flowers are deep pink, borne in drooping clusters. For a dark leaved companion of Canna ehmani nothing is finer than Canna King Humbert. This plant grows four feet in height, with leaves of a dark green bronze color—a very striking plant for massing. Among other useful varieties are Queen Helene, growing five feet high, flowers having a yellow ground blotched with red; Uncle Sam, seven feet with brilliant orange scarlet flowers; Wyoming with orange flowers, the plant growing to a height of seven feet and having large, purple foliage. The Cannas named are selected for their large leaves and tall growth; all bear large, beautiful flowers.

CALATHEA ZEBRINA—Maranta zebrina

Another class of plants with large, tropical leaves are the Colocasias. Colocasia odorata grows to a height of ten feet, and has beautiful green leaves, measuring in well-grown plants two feet six inches by three feet six inches. The leaves point upward and not downward, as in Colocasia esculenta, the common Elephants-ear. The latter will grow to a height of six feet and has dark green leaves two feet six inches by four feet.

Cyperus papyrus (Egyptian Paper Plant) is also a very interesting plant and one that should be in every water garden, especially where the Lotus is grown. It attains a height of ten feet; on the end of the stalks is a tuft of long, threadlike leaves which gives the plant a very graceful and striking appearance. It thrives well planted in shallow water, or in the border, given the same treatment as the Canna. It is tender and should not be exposed to severe freezing; on the approach of frost the plant should be potted and wintered in the greenhouse, where it can be kept in a growing condition. It can be increased by division of the roots or by seed sown in spring. It looks best when in clumps of several plants, set about a foot apart. See photograph, page 73.

SUBTROPICAL PLANTS AT WATER'S EDGE

CYPERUS ALTERNIFOLIUS
The Umbrella-sedge

Cyperus alternifolius (Umbrella-sedge) does well in like conditions to the preceding. The plant grows from one and one-half to three and one-half feet in height, having the same tufted head as Cyperus papyrus, only the leaves in alternifolius are much wider, being from one-quarter to one-half inch in width. This and its two varieties, Cyperus alternifolius gracilis, with finer leaves, and Cyperus alternifolius variegata, with beautiful variegated stems and leaves, should be wintered in the greenhouse.

Fatsia papyrifera (sometimes named Aralia papyrifera) grows from five to seven feet high; the leaves are cordate, five to seven lobed, about one foot in length and the same in width. This is the plant from which the Japanese make rice paper. It is semi-hardy in sheltered locations around Washington, D. C, sending up shoots from the roots. Farther north the plants should be lifted after the first touch of frost and wintered in a cool greenhouse.

Monstera deliciosa is a very interesting plant, with large leaves. It bears an edible fruit which has a taste resembling that between a banana and a pineapple. The fruit is from six to eight inches long and in form resembles a pine cone. The leaves are from one to two feet six inches in length, fifteen to eighteen inches wide, are perforated and the margins deeply cut. This plant succeeds well in the border and frequently bears fruit. At the approach of frost the plant should be potted and brought into the greenhouse or dwelling. It makes a fine house plant for winter decoration.

FATSIA PAPYRIFERA

Musa ensete, the Abyssinian Banana, is one of the best tropical plants to use for this purpose. It is a noble subject, easily raised frornseed, which should be sown in the greenhouse or hotbed. The young plants grow rapidly and within three years will attain a height of ten feet, with leaves cightjfeet in length and two feet wide.

Musa sapientum is another banana that is very interesting; it grows to a height of twelvc feet, the old plants flowering and bearing fruit which, however, owing to our short summers, will not reach maturity in the Northern States.

Musa martini is similar to the preceding; the veins and slems are gcnerally tinted red, while the leaves are thick and not easily broken by the wind.

Musa dacca is smaller growing and can, therefore, be planted toward the edge of the border.

Musa vittata has green leaves, beautifully striped and blotched with white; this is one of the finest of variegated plants.

Musa zebrina has dark green leaves blotched and striped with purplish bronze.

Nicotiana tomentosa, or as it is better known to gardeners, Nicotiana colossea, is well described by its more popular name. Colossal it certainly is, growing to a height of nine feet, with leaves two feet six inches by fifteen inches wide, furnished to the ground. It forms a picture in itself. This tobacco is a perennial, flowering the second year in the North; if the plant is wintered in the greenhouse it can be raised from cuttings of soft unripened wood taken in the fall; or from seed sown in the greenhouse or hotbed in the spring.

MUSA ENSETE The Abyssinian Banana

Ricinus zanzibariensis (Castor-oil-plant), with its immense leaves three feet from point to point, and the plant fifteen feet in height, is a splendid subject for the back row of the border where it will tower above the lower plants in front. It should be raised from seed sown in spring in a greenhouse or hotbed.

Strelitzia Augusta does well in the border and has a very tropical appearance. It grows to a height of fifteen feet. The leaves are two to three feet in length, borne on petioles four feet long. The plant has to be wintered in the greenhouse.

Where shade can be provided, the Australian Tree Fern, Alsophila australis, thrives very well in the subtropical border. It makes a quick growth, throwing out its large, beautiful fronds rapidly. These measure seven feet from stem to point of frond and four feet across. This plant should be potted at the approach of frost and wintered in the greenhouse.

Solanum warscewiczi, growing to a height of ten feet, with large, deeply lobed leaves eighteen inches across, forms a very striking plant. It is easily raised from seed which should be sown in spring.

Solanum robustum grows four feet high; the leaves are not as large nor so deeply lobed as those of the last mentioned. It forms a nice, compact plant. Both of the Solanums can be raised from seed sown in spring or from cuttings taken in the fall.

Xanthosoma sagittaefolium is also a very desirable plant; the leaves are over two feet across and about three feet in length, with a beautiful metallic luster on the upper surface, which makes it a very attractive plant.

Another Xanthosoma very similar to the preceding is Xanthosoma violaceum. This variety lacks the luster on the surface of the leaf possessed by Xanthosoma sagittaefolium, but has very beautiful violet colored stems.

All of the plants named, unless where noted, should be taken up after frost has injured the leaves, making them unsightly, the leaves cut off and the plants put into as small pots as possible and carried through the winter in a cool greenhouse. If a greenhouse be not available they can be lifted and stood in a corner of a frostproof cellar, and the roots covered with a layer of sand which should be kept moist but not too wet; Cannas can be lifted and carried over in this manner.

Chapter XVII

HARDY PERENNIALS FOR MARGIN AND BORDER PLANTING

IT will add very much to the beauty of the natural or semi-natural pond or stream to plant the edges with some of the hardy subjects hereinafter described. The edge of the pond can be planted with a selection of hardy herbaceous plants flowering at different periods, thus providing an attraction from early spring to late fall. These plants should be set out in colonies, several of one variety together, wherever space is at command to allow of this being done. They can be planted in front of the hardy trees and shrubs used as wind-breaks. Many of them, such as Acorus, Typha, Juncus, Peltandra, the Saggitarias and the Pontederia, can be placed on the edge of the bank and allowed to extend out into the pond in the shallow water. All of the plants named will grow well on the bank or in the water. In all such plantings it is well to bear in mind the fact that the water garden is the principal object, and the other plants only a setting for it; therefore, all the space at the edge should not be planted, but open spots reserved where one can get right down to the water to see the lilies. The plants named have either beautiful flowers, attractive foliage, or striking habit of growth to recommend them, and are, therefore, especially desirable, although they form but a partial enumeration of a very long list of hardy plants that would succeed equally as well. It would be an extensive pond indeed where all of the plants available could be employed in the borders surrounding it; the list given is to serve merely as a guide to the prospective purchaser who may select from it those that best serve the purpose in view.

Acorus calamus (Sweetflag) grows to a height of from two to three feet; it has lance-shaped leaves. All parts of the plant have a strong, aromatic, acrid taste and the rhizome is much used in medicine and by perfumers.

Acorus calamus variegatus (A. japonica variegata) has, in the young state, leaves striped deep yellow, which fade to a paler color as they become older.

Acorus gramineus grows to a height of from eight to twelve inches, forming a round, grassy tuft.

Acorus gramineus variegatus is a beautiful variegated plant. The leaves are narrow, grasslike and striped white. All of the Acorus will thrive equally well planted in moist soil or in shallow water. They are propagated by division of the root in spring or fall.

Acanthus mollis latifolius has leaves one foot wide by two feet long. It grows to a height of from three to four feet and is a fine, hardy plant for subtropical effect. It should be planted in well-drained soil and well mulched to protect it in winter from frost. It is propagated by division in spring and fall.

Anemone rivularis produces white flowers with a purple disk; it attains a height of from eighteen to twenty inches and delights in a moist situation. Propagation is effected by division of the crowns, or root cuttings, also by seed sown as soon as ripe, or in spring.

Anagallis tenella is a plant of trailing habit, rarely reaching a height of more than six inches. The flowers are bright pink, the plants blooming freely for several months in summer. It is propagated by division or from cuttings of the young shoots.

Hardy Asters

Aster novae-angliae reaches a height of from four to five feet; it bears bluish purple flowers with yellow centers, and blooms through September and October.

Aster novae-angliae alba reaches a height of four feet; its flowers are white.

Aster novae-angliae rosea grows four feet high, and has bright rose colored flowers.

Aster novae-angliae rubra grows four feet high, bearing deep rose colored flowers.

Colwell Pink. A fine, pink flowered variety; flowers of medium size, produced in great profusion during the month of September. The plant is a vigorous grower of upright habit.

Saturn. Bears beautiful pale blue flowers of large size. This is one of the best of the newer varieties.

White Climax. Pure white flowers of large size, centers golden yellow; plant of strong, erect habit and free in bloom.

Robertson V. C. Semi-double flowers of pale violet color; plant of strong erect habit; very free in flower.

Peggy Ballard. Flowers of rosy lilac color, semi-double; plant of vigorous growth and upright habit; one of the best of the Asters.

Sam Banham. A splendid new white-flowered Aster of recent introduction. The flowers average two inches in diameter, borne on strong, upright stems four to five feet in height, and blooming during August and September.

All these Asters delight in deep, moist soil, exposed to full sunshine. The plants are very effective in the late fall months when covered with their showy, attractive flowers. They can be grown from seed sown in spring or by division of the roots in spring or fall.

Astilbe rivularis (Spiraea) has foliage very similar to Spiraea aruncus. The flowers are whitish, tinted red. The plant bears many flowered panicles and grows to a height of from three to four feet in wet soil. It blooms during July and August and is propagated by division of the crowns.

Astilbe rubra has deep pink flowers.

Astrantia carniolica produces beautiful white flowers; the plant grows to a height of twelve inches.

Astrantia helleborifolia gives light pink flowers; it grows to a height of two feet.

Astrantia major has rosy pink flowers and grows to a height of from eighteen inches to two feet.

BOCCONIA CORDATA
Hardy Border Plant

The Astrantias like plenty of moisture and do well in wet soil. They are propagated by division of the root in fall or spring.

Bocconia cordata grows to a height of from five to eight feet; the leaves are large, heart-shaped, deeply lobed, silvery white underneath. The plant bears a large panicle of yellowish white flowers and is an excellent subject for the banks and borders of the pond. Being perfectly hardy and growing rapidly from suckers it soon forms a beautiful specimen. It likes a good, deep soil that is well drained and therefore should not be planted where the soil is marshy. It is increased by division of the roots, from suckers, and from seed sown as soon as ripe or in the spring.

Buphthalmum speciosum (Telekia speciosa) is a perennial plant, with large, showy yellow flowers, growing to a height of from three to four feet. It has large, cordate, coarse, serrate leaves. Propagation is by division in fall or spring.

Butomus umbellatus (Floweringrush) bears rose colored flowers. The leaves resemble those of the Iris, and are from two to three feet in length. It should be planted at the margin of the pond or in shallow water. It is propagated by division.

Caltha leptosepala gives pure white flowers; it grows to a height of from twelve to fifteen inches, blooming from spring till June.

Caltha palustris (Marshmari-gold) reaches a height of from one to two feet, and bears bright yellow flowers half an inch across.

Caltha palustris monstrosa plena has larger flowers than the type; they are double.

The Calthas thrive best in a wet location or in a moist border. They are propagated by division of the roots early in Spring or after flowering.

Cardamine pratensis flore pleno grows luxuriantly in wet soil, flowering freely during the spring months. The flower stalks reach a height of from fifteen to twenty inches. The color of the flowers is light blue with a touch of deep purple. Increased by division.

Chelone glabra reaches a height of from one to two feet; the flowers are white, being often tinted rose.

Chelone lyoni grows about two feet high and bears rosy purple flowers.

Chelone obliqua (Turtlehead) grows to a height of from one to two feet. The flowers are deep rose, borne in close terminal spikes.

The Chelones like wet soil and do not thrive in dry locations; they flower freely and keep on blooming until late summer. They are increased by dividing the plants in fall, by seed, and by cuttings of the young wood.

Clematis paniculata is a splendid vine to run over a rock, stump, or to ramble over a rustic bridge or tree. It is the best of the small flowered Clematises, often growing, when well established, fifteen feet in a single season. The flowers are borne in the

CLEMATIS PANICULATA
The flowers are borne in the greatest profusion, forming a dense white mass of fragrant blossoms

greatest profusion, forming a dense white mass of fragrant blossoms. It blooms in August, remaining in good condition for several weeks. Propagation is effected by seed sown outdoors in fall when ripe, or in a cool greenhouse or frame.

Commelina virginica is a beautiful native plant, excellent for naturalizing purposes. The flowers are pale sky blue in color. It should be planted in damp, rich soil, and is propagated by seed or cuttings.

DICENTRA SPECTABILIS
The Bleedingheart of the old-fashioned garden

Dicentra spectabilis, the Bleedingheart of the old-fashioned garden, is a plant that should always be included. It thrives well in a light, rich soil, moist but not wet, and especially prefers a partially shaded location. The plant reaches a height of from one to two feet. The flowers are borne in a graceful raceme, are rosy crimson in color, about one inch long, heart-shaped, appearing in spring. This is one of the best hardy perennial plants in cultivation. It is propagated by division, or by cutting the roots into small pieces and inserting them in sandy soil.

Digitalis purpurea, the old-fashioned English Foxglove, should have a position in the hardy border. It succeeds best in a light, rich, moist soil andgrows from two feet six inches to four feet in height. The color of the flowers ranges from white to purple.

Digitalis purpurea gloxiniaeflora is a stronger, more robust plant than the type; the flower spike is larger, the flowers, which are prominently spotted, opening wider. It can be increased by division and by seed sown in the fall or spring, in a sheltered location.

DIGITALIS PURPUREA
The Foxglove. A favorite plant for the hardy border

Dipsacus sylvestris grows to a height of from five to six feet. It is a biennial plant and bears pale lilac flower heads.

Dipsacus fullonum is similar to the preceding, with the exception that the floral scales are hooked. It is raised from seed.

Ferula communis is a plant with very finely divided leaves; it grows to a height of from eight to twelve feet. The flowers are yellow, appearing in umbels of forty to fifty small blossoms. It has beautiful fernlike foliage and thrives well in ordinary soil, or at the water's edge. It is easily raised from seed.

Funkia subcordata also thrives well in moist soil near the margin of the pond. The leaves are from six to nine inches long, broadly cordate-ovate. The flowers are pure white, from four to six inches in length, and from three to five inches broad, bell-shaped; borne in spikes carrying from nine to fifteen flowers, the spike one and one-half to two feet high. They bloom in July and August.

Funkia fortunei bears pale lilac flowers and grows to a height of from eighteen inches to two feet. It is propagated by division of the crowns in spring.

There is a fine variegated one, Funkia ovata marginata, the leaves of which have a broad white margin. The flowers are bluish lilac.

Gunnera manicata has gigantic leaves from five to ten feet across, on long prickly petioles. The leaves are orbicular, lobed and crenate; the flowers are green on a dense spike three to four feet tall.

GUNNERA SCABRA
A noble plant when once established

Gunnera scabra is smaller than the preceding, with leaves four to five feet in diameter on strong, prickly petioles three to six feet in length.

The Gunneras thrive best in moist soil and will stand the winters in the northern states if protected with leaves or straw. They are noble plants when once established, but will not thrive in dry soil. They are propagated by division of the roots.

Helenium autumnale produces flowers ranging in color from yellow to deep orange with a yellow disk. It grows to a height of from three to six feet, flowering from July to October.

Helenium autumnale superbum has much larger flowers than the type and grows from four to six feet high. The flowers are deep golden yellow.

Helenium autumnale var. pumilum flowers profusely from July until October, reaching a height of eighteen inches.

Helenium grandicephalum striatum is of strong, robust habit, growing to a height of three feet. The flowers measure one and one-half inches across and are of a deep orange color striped and blotched with crimson. Its blooming period is from July to August.

The Heleniums are quite at home in the moist soil surrounding the pond, and are very showy when in flower. They are propagated by division or seed.

Helianthus giganteus (Indian-potato) grows to a height of from four to twelve feet. The lanceolate leaves are from three to seven inches long; flowers pale yellow, one and one-half to three inches in diameter. This plant is quite at home in wet soil.

Hemerocallis flava gives beautiful, single, lemon yellow flowers, which grow stems of a height of from two to three feet. The leaves are narrow, from two to two and one-half feet in length.

Hemerocallis fulva has single orange colored flowers; it blooms in June and July, attaining a height of from three to four feet.

Hemerocallis fulva kwanso gives double orange colored flowers, remaining in bloom for a longer period than Hemerocallis fulva. It grows to a height of three feet.

Hemerocallis fulva variegata has a white stripe down the center of the leaves.

All the Hemerocallis should be planted where they can be afforded plenty of water. They are found growing wild along the edges of streams and in wet places. Propagation is effected by division of the roots.

Heracleum villosum (H. giganteum) reaches a height of from eight to twelve feet. It has pinnate leaves and greenish white flowers borne in dense umbels; flowering in August and September. This is a plant well adapted for use at the pond or in the surrounding border. It is increased by division or seed.

Hibiscus Crimson Eye is a clear white flower, with a crimson eye.

Hibiscus moscheutos (Rosemallow) grows from three to four feet high and bears flowers four to six inches across, of a light rose color, in August and September.

Hibiscus moscheutos albus is similar to the preceding, except in the color of the flower, which is white with a purple eye.

Hibiscus militaris grows from three to four feet high. The flowers measure from three to five inches across, ranging in color from white to pale rose with a purple eye.

The Hibiscus named delight in wet soil and are very effective with their large bright flowers and strong growth. They are easily raised from seed sown in early spring.

Iris aurea produces yellow flowers, on from three to three and one-half foot stems, in June.

HEMEROCALLIS FULVA

Iris caroliniana has leaves of from two to three feet in length; the flowers are lilac, variegated with purple and brown.

Iris laevigata (kaempferi) delights in rich wet soil, where the plants will grow to a height of four and one-half feet. When they flower, in June and July, there is nothing in hardy plants that can rival them in the gorgeous colors of the blossoms which frequently measure twelve inches across. They have both double and single flowers, the colors of which range from white, lilac and crimson purple to the deepest purple imaginable. Some have variegated or spotted flowers. All of the blossoms have a pure yellow center. The plants grow well at the edge of the water, and thrive equally well when planted in shallow water. They appear to best advantage when planted in large groups instead of singly. Unfortunately, the names of this class of Iris are badly confused; therefore, a list of varieties is of very little benefit to intending purchasers. It is best to visit some nursery when the plants are in flower and then select the varieties desired.

Iris Monnieri gives lemon-yellow flowers and reaches a height of from three to three and one-half feet.

Iris orientalis bears white and yellow flowers and grows to a height of from three to four feet.

Iris pseudacorus has yellow flowers, the outer segments being from two to two and one-half inches in length. The plants grow to a height of from two to three feet, forming fine, large clumps. They flower in May and June.

Iris pseudacorus pallida gives pale yellow flowers.

Iris pseudacorus variegata has leaves striped with creamy white.

Iris versicolor grows from one and one-half to two feet high, the limb being violet blue; there is a yellow variegation on the claw and veined with purple.

These Irises delight in wet soil, where they will soon make fine clumps that will flower profusely every year.

None of the German Irises likes wet soil, but if a bank or some well-drained spot can be had, then a generous planting of this class should be carried out. All have very attractive flowers, some of the newer ones rivaling the orchids in the wonderful gradations of the colors.

Juncus effusus spiralis has curiously twisted stems in the form of a corkscrew.

Juncus effusus vittatus has the foliage barred with bands of yellow.

The Juncus, or Rush, is very useful for planting in shallow water or at the edge of the pond. The plants are increased by division of the root.

Lobelia cardinalis (Cardinalflower) grows from two to four feet high. The flowers are bright, intense cardinal red, borne on a long spike. This is one of the finest of our native plants and should be largely used around the pond. It delights in wet soil, flowering from July to September.

Lobelia fulgens also throws a fine, brilliant scarlet flower, much like that of Lobelia cardinalis, blooming from four to five weeks earlier than the latter. All are propagated by seed or division.

Lobelia syphilitica grows to a height of from two to three feet; the flowers range in color from blue to purple.

MERTENSIA VIRGINICA
The Virginian Cowslip or Bluebell

Lobelia syphilitica alba has flowers nearly white.

Lysimachia clethroides grows from two to three feet high. The flowers are white, borne on long spikes. It blooms from July to September, growing splendidly in wet places. Propagation is effected by division of the root in spring or fall.

Malva alcea reaches a height of from two to four feet. The flowers are pale rosy purple, two inches across. The leaves are palmate, light green and deeply incised. This plant makes a fine clump when well established, growing as much in diameter as it does in height.

Malva moschata (Muskmallow) produces rose colored flowers, two inches across in terminal and axillary clusters. The lower leaves are kidney-shaped, the upper ones form five deeply pinnatifid segments. It grows to a height of from two to two and one-half feet.

All the Malvas thrive in a moist soil and are propagated by seed or cuttings. Menyanthes trifoliata (Buckbean) produces flowers which are white inside, the outside being reddish colored and the anthers purplish. This plant grows well in shallow water or in moist soil. It is propagated by division of the root.

Mertensia virginica (Virginian Cowslip or Bluebell) grows from one to two feet in height, producing drooping clusters of blue bell flowers. The buds on first opening are tinted pink, changing to clear blue; the flowers are one inch in length, borne in graceful, drooping terminal clusters. It blooms from April to May and is one of the most charming of hardy plants, delighting in deep, rich, moist soil. When once planted it should be disturbed as little as possible.

Mertensia sibirica comes into flower a little later than the preceding, the flowers being a lighter blue. The plant grows from one to two feet high. It is propagated by division, or by seed sown as soon as ripe.

Molopospermum cicutarium is a handsome, fernlike perennial, growing to a height of from three to five feet. Its yellowish white flowers are produced in umbels, the terminal umbel being very much larger than the lateral. It grows well in deep, rich soil where it can be well supplied with water. Propagation is by division, or seed can be sown as soon as ripe.

Myosotis palustris (true Forget-me-not) has decumbent stems from six to eighteen inches long. Its blossoms are borne in a loose flowered raceme, being bright blue with a yellow eye and appearing in May and June.

Myosotis palustris semperflorens is a dwarfer plant than the last mentioned, flowering nearly all summer.

The Forget-me-nots should be planted in a moist, shady location. They are easily propagated from seed, cuttings, or by division of the plants in the spring.

Peltandra undulata (Water-arum) has narrow, sagitate leaves, glossy green; the spathe is from four to eight inches long.

Peltandra alba has broader leaves than the preceding; the flower spathe is white.

The Water-arums are attractive plants for the edge of the pond, their dark, glossy green, sagittate leaves being very effective. They are propagated by separating the plants and from seed.

Polygala lutea (Orange Milkwort) is a native plant found wild in many of the Eastern States. It is quite at home in moist soil and should never be allowed to suffer from dryness. The flowers are orange yellow in color, appearing from June to October. The plant reaches a height of from six to twelve inches, and is propagated from seed sown in fall or spring.

PELTANDRA UNDULATA — Water-arum

Pontederia cordata (Pickerelweed) is one of the handsomest of aquatic plants for shallow water. It is found growing wild in almost every natural pond, or pool, all over the Eastern States, and might with justice be termed a weed; still it is worthy of a place in any pond devoted to the growth of aquatic plants, being very attractive when in bloom. It is a strong growing perennial, standing in clumps and sending up strong stems of from two to three feet in height. The flowers are light blue. Propagation is effected by division of the tufts.

Pyrethrum uliginosum (Giant Ox-eye Daisy) is well adapted for the moist border or margin. It is a bold, strong growing, handsome species. The flowers have white rays with a yellow disk and measure from two to three inches across, being borne on slender stalks. The plant grows to a height of from four to five feet. Its flowering period is from July to September. Propagation is by division. This is one of the noblest of herbaceous plants; the blooms are excellent for cut flowers.

Rheum officinale (Rhubarb) is a strong, robust plant. The leaves are from eighteen inches to three feet across, with three to seven lobes extending to nearly one-half of the leaf. The flower stem grows to a height of from three to five feet and bears a large panicle of greenish white blossoms.

Rheum emodi is another fine foliage plant, growing to a height of five feet with beautiful, large leaves having prominent red veins.

The Rheums like a well drained soil where they will never suffer from lack of moisture; they are well adapted for the border or margin. The crowns should be well protected by a covering of leaves, or brush, in winter. Propagation is by division, or seed.

Rhexia virginica (Meadowbeauty) is another moisture loving, low, tuberous-rooted plant, growing from six to twelve inches high, and flowering from July to September. The flowers are bright rosy purple with golden anthers.

PONTEDERIA CORDATA
Pickerelweed

PYRETHRUM ULIGINOSUM—Giant Ox-eye
Daisy One of the noblest of herbaceous plants

Rhexia lutea has yellow flowers.

Rhexia mariana gives reddish purple flowers, which open a little earlier than those of Rhexia virginica. All delight in wet, spongy soil, and are increased by division of the roots.

Rudbeckia laciniata and its better known offspring, Rudbeckia laciniata flora plena (Goldenglow) are fine plants for the border surrounding the pond. They grow to a height of from five to six feet, bearing golden yellow flowers which appear from July to September. Rudbeckia Goldenglow is one of the best hardy plants for the border.

Rudbeckia nitida (Autumn Glory) produces large pale yellow flowers, opening through August and September. The plant grows to a height of five feet. These Rudbeckias must have plenty of water to bring them to perfection, and should be replanted at least every three years. Owing to the rapid spread of the crown they soon become exhausted if not renewed. They are easily raised from division of the root either in spring or fall.

Sagittaria sagittaefolia (Arrowhead) is a perennial plant much used for the edge of ponds. It succeeds well planted in shallow water or at the edge in wet soil. The leaves are broad, sagittate, from two to eight inches in length. The flower stems are erect, from six to eight inches long, and are carried a little above the leaves. The flowers are white, from half an inch to one inch across.

Sagittaria latifolia (Variabilis) is variable as to height, growing from a few inches up to three or four feet. The leaves are generally broad, sagittate with long basal lobes; the flowers are white, one inch across.

Sagittaria japonica flora plena is very similar to the preceding, bearing large spikes of pure white, double flowers.

Sagittaria montevidensis (Giant Arrowhead) is a strong, robust plant, attaining a height of from four to five feet. The leaves are fifteen inches in length, the flower heads being carried on long stems well above the foliage. The roots of this variety should be planted below the reach of frost or it will be killed outright. It is increased by division.

Sabbatia chloroides grows from one to two feet high and is a biennial. The flowers are white, two inches across. It thrives in wet, boggy soil and is raised from seed.

Sanguisorba canadensis bears greenish white flower heads from two to six inches in length. The plant grows to a height of from five to six feet and well deserves a place in the border.

Saxifraga peltata is a bold, strong growing plant, perfectly at home in moist locations. The leaves are from six to eight inches in diameter; the flowers are whitish pink, borne on stalks from one to two feet high. The plant blooms in the spring months, and succeeds best in deep rich, moist soil. Propagation is effected by seed or division.

Scirpus lacustris grows to a height of from three to eight feet, in low, wet marshy places, or in shallow water.

Scirpus lacustris zebrina, commonly called the Porcupine Plant from the markings of the leaves, is of strong, robust, upright growth, reaching a height of from three to four feet. The leaves are variegated with alternate bands of white, the bands being almost half an inch wide. This is a very effective subject, planted in shallow water or at the edge of the pond. It is propagated by division.

Spiraea aruncus (Goatsbeard Spiraea) is a perennial plant growing from three to five feet high., with beautiful divided leaves. It bears large white, gracefully drooping plumes, blooming from June to July.

Spiraea gigantea reaches a height of from five to six feet. The leaves are palmate. The flower spike is extra large, white, the flowering period being from July to September.

Spiraea kneiffi has finely divided leaves, and produces large panicles of silvery white flowers in June; it grows from three to four feet in height.

The Spiraeas named delight in deep, rich, moist soil, and succeed well planted at the water's edge. They are propagated by division of the roots.

Thalia dealbata is a plant with glaucous foliage somewhat like that of the Canna. It grows to a height of from three to five feet. The leaves are from six to nine inches in length, on petioles of from one to four feet. The flower panicle is borne on stems from three to five feet high, having many very small purple flowers. The plant blooms from June to September.

Thalia divaricata grows to a height of from five to ten feet, and is larger in all its parts than Thalia dealbata. The flowers are purple.

The Thalias are very interesting plants, succeeding best planted in shallow water or wet soil. They also do well accorded the same treatment as Cannas. They have proved perfectly hardy, without any protection at Washington, D. C., for a number of years. The plants are increased by division or seed.

SPIRAEA ARUNCUS
Goatsbeard Spiraea. Bears large white, gracefully drooping plumes

THALIA DEALBATA
One of the finest subjects for waterside planting. Broad, cannalike, glaucous leaves, with panicles of purplish flowers. The plant is hardy as far north as Philadelphia in sheltered locations

Trilliums delight in moist, deep rich soil. They should be given a shady position. The best one for the margin of the pond is Trillium grandiflorum, which grows to a height of from one to two feet. The leaves are broad-ovate, from three to five inches long. The flowers are three-petaled, pure white on first opening, changing to rose pink, and measure two inches across. This Trillium is a beautiful plant, of free growth in a shady position, but will not grow where it is exposed to the full sun. It is increased by the division of the root, or seed.

Trollius europaeus (Globeflower) is a hardy perennial plant bearing pale yellow flowers from one to one and one-half inches in diameter. It reaches a height of from one to two feet.

Trollius thrives best in deep, wet soil. They are handsome, erect growing plants, of dense habit, flowering from May to July, and are propagated by division or seeds.

Typha latifolia (Cattail) grows from four to eight feet high, flowering on a close, round, dark brownish black spike from four to nine inches in length.

Typha angustifolia is more slender in leaf and flower spike than Typha latifolia, and is the more graceful of the two, growing from five to ten feet high.

The Typhas are hardy perennial water or bog plants; a clump of them, especially when in flower, forms a very attractive object in the water garden. They are increased by division and seed.

AN AMATEUR'S WATER GARDEN

Chapter XVIII

NATIVE ORCHIDS, SARRACENIAS, AND OTHER BOG PLANTS

THE native orchids generally delight in a shady position. Some like the soil well drained, while others are bog plants and delight in an abundant supply of moisture.

Arethusa bulbosa is a beautiful native orchid, found wild in wet, boggy swamps in North Carolina. The flowers are bright rosy pink, appearing in May and June. It should be planted in a shady corner where it will have an abundance of water. It is propagated by the separation of the bulbs.

Calopogon puchellus is a hardy native orchid found in wet, boggy places. The flowers are one inch in diameter, pink in color, bearded with white, yellow, and purple hairs. The flowers come in clusters of from two to six. This orchid should be planted in a place where it will have full exposure to the sun.

Calypso borealis is a pretty native orchid with rosy pink flowers; the lip is white with brown spots. This plant does best in light, rich, wet soil, and should be planted in a cool, shady spot.

Cypripedium acaule (Ladyslipper) has a large, solitary flower, borne on a stem from eight to twelve inches high. The flower is of a rosy purple color. The plant likes a moist location.

Cypripedium parviflorum (Small Yellow Ladyslipper) grows about twelve inches high, thriving well in moist soil and flowering from May to July.

Cypripedium pubescens (Large Yellow Ladyslipper) flowers in May and June. It has large, yellow flowers, spotted with brown; the lip is pale yellow. It thrives well in wet soil or in low places in the woods.

Cypripedium spectabile or reginae is the showiest and finest of the hardy Cypripediums. It grows from one and one-half to two feet in height, thriving well in open, moist woods, meadows and peat bogs. The flowers are white with a large blotch of rosy carmine in front of the labellum.

Cypripedium spectabile album is a pure white form of the preceding.

All the Cypripediums should be well supplied with peat or leafmold, and theroots planted deep in the soil. Asurface dressing of sphagnum moss will act as a mulch and retain the moisture when the plants are in dry soil.

Habenaria blephariglottis grows from one to two feet high, and bears beautiful fringed white flowers. It does well in wet boggy soil.

Habenaria bracteata reaches a height of from eight to twelve inches. It thrives well in a moist, shady position, and bears small greenish flowers.

CYPRIPEDIUM REGINAE—Spectabile
Copyrighted by H. P. Kelsev, Salem, MA.

Habenaria ciliaris (Yellow Fringed Orchid) produces bright orange yellow flowers with a distinct fringe. It does well in boggy soil.

Habenaria dilatata grows about twelve inches high, has leafy stems, and produces small white flowers. It thrives well in wet bogs.

Habenaria fimbriata gives long spikes of lilac purple flowers also distinctly fringed. It delights in wet soil.

SARRACENIA FLAVA—Pitcher Plant
Suitable for moist soil at edge of pond.
Hardy at Washington, D. C.

Habenaria psycodes has handsome purple, fragrant flowers, borne on a spike from five to ten inches in length. It should be planted in wet soil.

The Habenarias like a soil composed of equal parts leafmold or peat and sand, with a surface dressing of leaves or moss.

Pogonia ophioglossoides grows from five to ten inches high, and bears pale rose colored flowers, sometimes white. It thrives in sphagnum moss or leafmold, in wet locations, flowering from June to July.

Spiranthes cernua (Nodding Ladies-tresses) reaches a height of from six to eighteen inches, and bears a dense spike of white flowers. It thrives well in moist, open soil.

Sarracenia drummondi has beautifully variegated pitchers from one to two feet in length. The hood is marked white, red and green; the white and purple flowers are from two to three inches across. This plant will not endure the winters of the northern states in the open.

Sarracenia flava has narrow pitchers two to two and one-half feet long, yellowish green.

SARRACENIA PURPUREA
Hardy anywhere in the United States

Sarracenia psittacina has small pitchers, about six inches in length; they are green below, purple with white spots above. This plant also requires to be wintered in the greenhouse.

Sarracenia purpurea (Common Pitcherplant) produces pitchers which attain a length of from eight to twelve inches, green colored, with purple veins; the flowers are borne on stems from one to two feet high, and are two inches across; the petals are bright purple. This is the hardiest of the pitcher plants native from Labrador to Florida.

Sarracenia rubra has pitchers from ten to fifteen inches in length, green with reddish veins; the flowers are reddish purple, three inches across.

Sarracenia variolaris produces a yellow flower about two inches wide; the pitchers measure from six to twelve inches in length, are yellowish white, variegated and veined with purple.

Sarracenias thrive under semi-aquatic conditions. They are found growing wild in swamps and low, wet ground, from Labrador to Florida.

All of the Sarracenias named are hardy at Washington, D. C. Sarracenia purpurea will prove hardy anywhere in the United States if given proper conditions, the others, if planted in a protected corner, and covered with leaves or brush in winter, should carry through without injury.

While the following are not pitcher plants, they require the same treatment, soil, etc., as are afforded these, and may well be described here:

Darlingtonia californica resembles the Sarracenias in many points, yet is quite distinct from them. Its leaves rise to a height of from one to two feet. The pitcher is slender, erect, and twisted, having a rounded head, with a large, triangular reddish tongue depending from the aperture. The ground color is light green, while the upper part is mottled with white and covered with reddish pink veins. This plant likes a soil composed of peat and sphagnum moss, and should be planted in a low, wet location. It is propagated by the separation of the side shoots. Darlingtonia californica

DIONAEA MUSCIPULA — Venus Flytrap
Delights in full sunlight and plenty of moisture

is not hardy in the Northern States and should be removed to the greenhouse; in warm sheltered corners it might survive the winters, if well protected by brush or leaves.

Dionaea muscipula (Venus Flytrap) is a very interesting native perennial plant found growing wild in North Carolina. The leaves are in pairs, joined, or hinged at the lower edge. On the upper edge of each leaf is a row of hairs closing on each other like a trap. On the inside of each leaf, toward its center, are three sensitive hairs that, if touched by an insect or other object, will cause the leaf to close up, imprisoning the insect or other intruder. The flowers are white, borne in terminal corymbs. The plant blooms from June to August. It will not stand the winters of the Northern States out of doors, yet it will well repay the little extra trouble of wintering it in a cool greenhouse. The Dionaea should be planted in wet soil where it will have an abundance of moisture and full exposure to the sun. It will also grow in the shade but not so vigorously. The soil best suited to its wants is a fine, fibrous peat with a surface dressing of sphagnum moss.

Drosera filiformis is a very interesting little native bog plant, with long, slender leaves which are covered with little glandular hairs. The flowers are purple rose. It grows to a height of one foot in wet, swampy ground.

Chapter XIX

HARDY FERNS

AMERICA is very fortunate in having from sixty to sixty-five species of ferns growing wild throughout the Northeastern and Middle States. The most beautiful of them are found in the swamps or along the streams that flow through woods where plenty of decaying humus is available.

All of the hardy ferns with a few exceptions prefer a cool, rich, light soil where they will be provided with an abundant supply of moisture and a well drained soil where the water will not stand and stagnate, but pass off freely. They like a soil of light fibrous material. The best results will be obtained from the use of two-thirds good leafmold, or peat, and one-third sand. The ferns will grow in any ordinary soil so long as their wants as to water and shade are supplied. They can be transplanted, with care, at any time of the year, but this should be done preferably in the spring or fall months. Some can be planted at the edge of the pond, others beneath trees or shrubs, while Polypodium vulgare, Asplenium trichomanes, Cheilanthes vestita, Nephrodium marginale and such like can be used in the crevices and fissures of the rocks or where the soil is thin and dry.

FINE CLUMPS OF FERNS, WELL SUITED FOR A SHADY BANK NEAR POND

DRYOPTERIS MARGINALIS—Leather Wood-
fern growing naturally in a fissure in the rocks

Adiantum pedatum (Hardy Maindenhair Fern) is found growing wild in deep moist soil in the valleys and low places of shady woods, where the soil has been washed down from the heights above. In such deep rich material the stem, or stipe, often grows to a height of two feet, with fronds from twelve to fifteen inches across.

Asplenium angustifolium (Narrow-leaved Spleenwort) is a fine fern, with light green, graceful fronds, growing from one to three feet in height. The fronds are divided, the divisions being from two to four inches long. It likes a moist, shady position.

Asplenium filixfemina (Lady Fern) is a handsome subject, growing to a height of two to three feet, with finely cut fronds. It should be planted in a moist location either in the sun or shade.

Botrychium virginianum is a native fern, growing about a foot high, with a broad, triangular frond. This fern likes a moist soil and a position where it will be shaded from the direct sunlight.

Botrychium obliquum (Ternatum) grows from six to twelve inches in height. It is not so finely divided as the preceding. It is suitable for open places.

Cystopteris bulbifera (Bladderfern) grows to a height of from one to two feet, and has long, narrow, slender fronds of light green color. It should have a moist, shady position.

Cystopteris fragilis is a smaller Fern, growing from four to eight inches high, with finely divided fronds. It should have a well-drained soil, in a shady position.

Dennstedtia punctilobula (Dicksonia pilosiuscula) is the Hay-scented Fern, and has long, thin, pale green fronds, growing to a height of from one to two feet. This fern will thrive in full sunlight, or in partially shady locations, doing well in moist soil that is well drained.

Dryopteris bootti is an intermediate form between Dryopteris cristatum and Dryopteris spinulosa, and is quite at home in a wet position. It grows from one to one and one-half feet high and has evergreen fronds. It should be planted in moist soil in a shady spot.

Dryopteris cristatum is found growing in wet, spongy soil in a shady place; it reaches to a foot in height, and has evergreen fronds.

Dryopteris cristatum clintoniana is a larger and more showy fern than the preceding; it also thrives in wet soil in a shady place, growing from two to three feet in height.

Dryopteris goldieana is one of the largest and strongest of the hardy ferns; the fronds are from two to four feet in length, and twelve to eighteen inches wide. It likes a shady, moist position.

Dryopteris marginalis (Leather Woodfern) is an evergreen fern, with deep green fronds from one to two feet in length and from three to five inches in width. It likes a moist, shady place. In the accompanying illustration it is seen growing in a fissure of a rock with the common Polypody and the Christmas Fern for companions.

Dryopteris thelypteris (Mashfern)

Dryopteris noveboracensis is a slender growing fern, about twelve inches in height; the fronds are from three to four inches wide. A rich, moist, shady position suits it best.

Dryopteris spinulosa is a fine evergreen fern, growing to a height of fifteen to eighteen inches, with fronds from three to four inches in width. It, too, should have a moist, shady place.

Dryopteris thelypteris (Marshfern) grows about twelve inches high; it has fronds two to three inches in width, and is found growing in open, sunny places in wet soil.

Lygodium palmatum (Hartford Fern) grows with a slender, twining stem from one to three feet in height. It likes a moist, shady position and should have some support. The crowns should be covered with leaves during winter to protect the plants from the frost.

Matteuccia struthiopteris (Onoclea struthiopteris) is commonly called the Ostrich Fern. The fronds grow from two to four feet high and from six to ten inches wide. It is a fine, graceful fern, succeeding well in shade or sunlight, in deep, rich soil.

Onoclea sensibilis (Sensitive Fern) is well suited for a wet position either in the sun or shade; it grows from one to three feet in height and has light green, triangular fronds, divided into oblong, lanceolate segments.

No. I—Adiantum pedatum (Maidenhair Fern). No. 2—Pteris aquilina (Bracken). No. 3—Phegopteris hexagonoptera (Winged Woodfern). No. 4—Polystichum acrostichoides (Christmas Fern). No. 5—Dryopteris marginalis—Aspidium marginale (Leather Woodfern). No. 6— Dryopteris cristatum (Crested Woodfern)

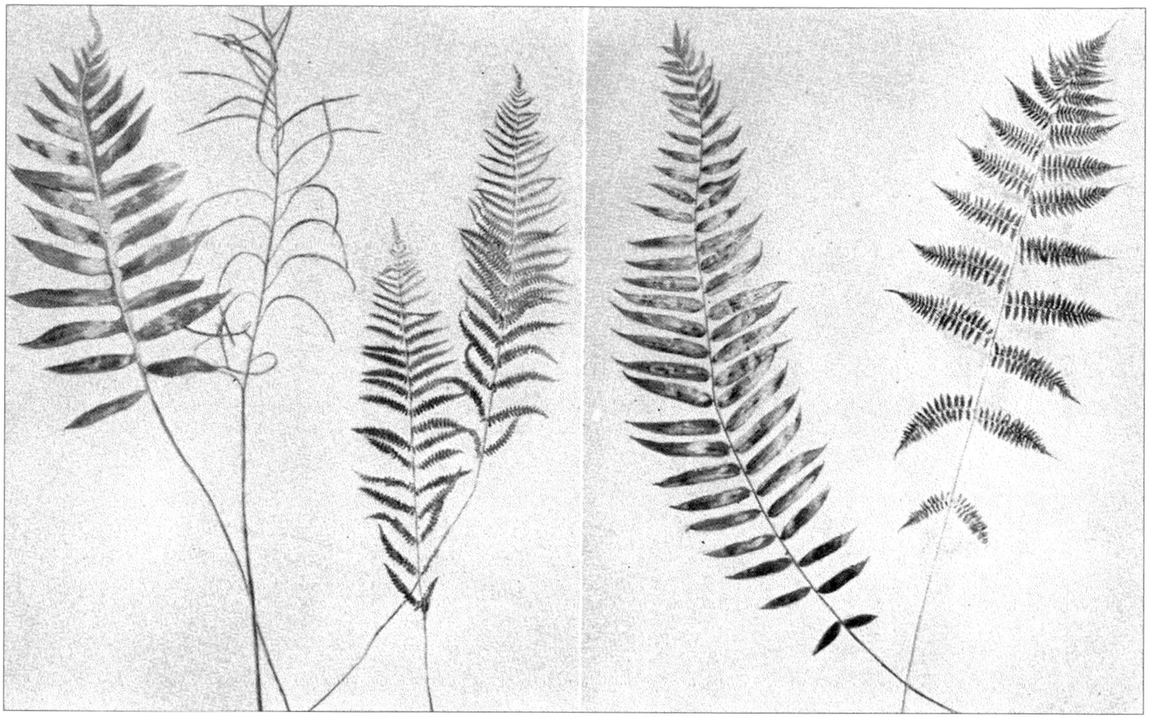

No. I   No. 2   No. 3   No. 4

No. 1 — Woodwardia areolata (W. angustifolia), sterile and fertile fronds (Chainfern.) No. 2 — Woodwardia (Virginia Chainfern). No. 3 — Asplenium angustifolium. No. 4 — Asplenium filix-femina

Ophioglossum vulgatum (Adderstongue fern) has a single leaf, growing from six to twelve inches in height, with a spike of spores at the apex. It likes a low wet position in the open.

Osmunda cinnamomea (Cinnamon Fern) is a beautiful plant, growing from three to five feet in height. The fronds are from six to eight inches wide; the stems when young are covered with a rusty down. It is quite at home in wet, swampy soil in sun or shade.

Osmunda claytoniana grows from two to three feet in height; it likes a dry, shady position.

Osmunda regalis (Royal Fern) is, without a doubt, the best fern for the edge of the pond. The accompanying illustration is reproduced from a photograph of a plant growing at the edge of a lily pond. The fern is perfectly hardy, growing from three to five feet in height; the fronds are pale green, nine to fifteen inches in width. It delights in a wet, swampy position, in peaty soil; but it will also do well in shallow water if the crown of the roots is above the surface.

Phegopteris dryopteris (Oakfern) is a pretty fern growing from nine to twelve inches high The triangular fronds are from three to five inches in width simply divided once or twice. It grows in shady places, in rich moist soil.

Phegopteris hexagonoptera (Winged Woodfern) is a fine subject for shady places, easily grown and quite showy; it makes fronds from seven to twleve inches wide, the plants growing about twelve inches high.

Phegopteris polypodioides has small, dark green fronds, growing about eight inches high, in moist, shady places.

Polypodium vulgare is a dainty evergreen fern, well suited for covering rocks. It grows in dense mats from four to ten inches high. It should have a partially shaded position. If planted in the open it should be placed where it will be well supplied with moisture.

Polystichum acrostichoides—Aspidium acrostichoides (Christmas Fern) is an evergreen fern, growing from eight to eighteen inches high with deep green fronds simply divided. It does best in a well-drained, shady position.

Pteris aquilina is the common Brake or Bracken, a large showy Fern, growing two to three feet in height, with large, triangular fronds. It likes a damp position in sun or shade.

Woodwardia areolata—syn. W. angustifolia (Chainfern) grows from nine to twelve inches high, and has fronds three to four inches wide. It likes a wet, swampy soil.

Woodwardia virginica grows from eighteen inches to two feet in height; the fronds are from three to five inches wide. This fern also will thrive in wet soil.

Chapter XX

ORNAMENTAL GRASSES AND BAMBOOS

ARUNDO DONAX MACROPHYLLA

THIS is a very interesting and useful class of plants for the decoration of the borders and margins of ponds. Some of the plants have green leaves and an upright habit of growth; others have leaves striped with white, and nearly all have a slender, airy, graceful habit that contrasts well with the broader foliage of other plants and trees.

The tallest of the grasses excepting the Bamboos, is the Arundo donax (Giant Reed), a perennial grass, growing to a height of from eight to twenty feet, according to soil and location. The flower plumes are from one to two feet in length, borne on loose, feathery spikes which are very showy. It may be of interest to the reader to know it is from the stems of this plant that musical reeds are made.

Arundo donax variegata is a smaller plant than the foregoing, growing not more than twelve feet in height. The leaves are striped white. It is not quite as hardy as the type and, therefore, should have a protected location. Both should be protected in the Northern States, through the winter months, with leaves or evergreen brush.

Arundo donax macrophylla glauca is a strong growing variety, with extra wide, dark, glossy green leaves, the underside of which are glaucous; the stems are very close jointed.

Arundo phragmites variegata is a fine plant for wet soil, growing to a height of from four to six feet, bearing a large, handsome panicle of purplish flowers. All of the Arundos are best increased by division of the crowns.

Among the bamboos the following will prove the hardiest. All of them should have their roots covered up with a good dressing of manure every fall, and on top of the manure a covering of tree leaves or evergreen boughs to protect them from frost. The height given is for the northern edge of the bamboo region. In a suitable climate, for instance, Phillostachys bambusoides reaches a height of sixty feet.

Arundinaria simoni is a fine plant, growing from ten to fifteen feet in height when well established; the leaves are from ten to twelve inches long, occasionally striped white.

Arundinaria japonica (Bambusa metake) has leaves of from eight to ten inches in length and one to two inches wide; the upper surface of a smooth glossy green; the lower side glaucous and rough.

Phyllostachys aurea (Bambusa aurea) will grow to a height of from fifteen to twenty feet when once established. The stems are yellow colored; the leaves light green. The plant has a light and graceful effect and is very suitable for the edge of the pond.

Phyllostachys henonis is one of the finest of this class of plants; a very graceful variety, with glossy green leaves. The young stems are green, turning to yellow as they become older. The plant grows to a height of from six to fifteen feet, according to soil and position; the leaves are two to three inches in length and about one-half inch in width.

Phyllostachys nigra (black-stemmed) grows from eight to fifteen feet high. The stems are first green, quickly turning to black as they get older. The leaves are from two to six inches in length, green above with a glaucous reverse.

Phyllostachys nigra punctata has yellow stems spotted black.

Phyllostachys bambusoides (quilioi) grows about eighteen feet high; the leaves are from six to eight inches long, one to one and three-quarters inches wide, dark green above and glaucous underneath.

Phyllostachys violascens grows to a height of ten to thirteen feet, and has dark purple stems changing to brownish yellow; the leaves are from three to six inches long.

PHYLLOSTACHYS AUREA—Bambusa aurea
At the commercial establishment of H. A. Dreer, Inc., Riverton, N. J.

Phyllostachys viridi-glaucescens is a beautiful, graceful bamboo, growing to a height of eighteen feet. The leaves are from three to four inches long and about one inch wide.

All the bamboos are propagated by division in Spring and, if possible, a ball of soil should be left with each division. Bamboos should be planted in some position where it will be possible to prevent the roots from extending to any great distance, or they will soon overrun other plants. To produce the best effect they should be grown in clumps of large size and kept as close and compact as possible.

Elymus canadensis glaucifolius is a strong perennial grass growing from three to five feet high; it has glaucous leaves from six to twelve inches in length. The flower spike is from four to nine inches long.

Elymus glaucus grows about three to four feet high, and has narrow, silvery glaucous foliage. The plants are propagated by division.

ERIANTHUS RAVENNAE

Erianthus ravennae is a beautiful hardy perennial grass of upright habit of growth. This plant resembles in habit of growth and flower plume the well known Pampasgrass. The leaves and stems are tinged with purple; the flower stems grow to a height of from five to ten feet. It should be planted in a deep rich soil with full exposure to the sun. It is propagated by seed and division.

Eulalia gracillimus (Eulalia gracillima univittata) has narrow green leaves with a narrow white stripe down the center of each. The plant grows from five to seven feet in height; the flower panicle is brown, large and showy. This is a very graceful variety, of beautiful, round, compact habit, the leaves drooping to the ground. It should be planted alone as a single specimen so as to develop its full beauty.

Eulalia japonica is a fine, hardy perennial grass from Japan, of strong, robust growth, reaching from six to nine feet in height. The flower panicle is brownish. The leaves are deep green, one and one-quarter inches wide, with a prominent white stripe down the center of each leaf; they are from two to three feet long.

Eulalia japonica zebrina is a variegated form of the preceding; its leaves are barred with alternate stripes of white and green.

Eulalia japonica variegata is dwarfer than those named. It grows to a height of from five to seven feet. The leaves are three-quarters of an inch wide and from one-half to two feet long; striped longitudinally with white; the stems are green and white tinted pink. See photograph page 129.

All of the Eulalias are best propagated by division of the roots in fall or spring. They can be raised from seed but rarely come true.

EULALIA GRACILLIMA UNIVITTATA
Plant well adapted for margin of pond

Gynerium argenteum (Pampasgrass) is a beautiful subject where it thrives well. It grows to a height of from eight to ten feet, and bears long, fluffy white plumes. Unfortunately it is rather tender, often suffering in our winters from frost. It should be planted in a sheltered nook, and protected by a covering of tree leaves and evergreen branches through the winter. The roots can also be taken up at the approach of frost, wintered in a cellar or cool greenhouse, and planted out early in spring; the plants will then commence to grow at once and will be sure to flower that season. It is propagated by division.

Molinia coerulea variegata is a small perennial grass with variegated foliage, very useful for edging or for the front row in the border. It grows from one to three feet high. The leaves are beautifully striped with white.

GYNERIUM ARGENTEUM—Pampasgrass
Grows to a height of from eight to ten feet and bears
long, fluffy white plumes

Panicum virgatum is a fine, hardy native grass, growing from three to four feet high. The leaves are twelve to fifteen'inches in length. The flower is purplish, borne on a tall branching panicle.

Panicum altissimum is similar to the preceding, growing from three to four feet high; it has dark brown flower panicles. The plants are propagated by division of the roots in spring or fall.

Phalaris arundinacea variegata (Reed Canary Grass) is a fine, low growing, variegated, hardy perennial grass, from two to three feet in height; the leaves are striped white.

Uniola latifolia is a native perennial grass, growing to a height of from three to four feet; it has large, loose drooping flower panicles.

EULALIA JAPONICA VARIEGATA

A beautiful grass with white stripes running lengthwise. The leaves of this plant make a fine display on the edge of a water garden

Chapter XXI

INSECTS, DISEASES, AND ENEMIES

THE water garden is not free from insect and other pests of various kinds; therefore, the same watchful care is required with waterlilies as in the case of other plants, so as to keep these enemies in check.

APHIDES

The black aphides will put in an appearance early in the year, especially when the weather is dry and hot with no rainfall. These insects will first be noticed on the leaf stems of the Nymphaeas and. Nelumbiums that rise above the water and, if not checked at this stage, they will soon spread over the leaves. The best way to destroy the aphides is to use the hose, or spray pump, with a good pressure of water, going over the plants carefully and knocking off the insects into the water where the gold fish will soon make short work of them. The force of the water will kill a great many of the aphides but, as some always escape and get on the plants again, these should be hosed once every day for two or three days or until the aphides are eradicated. Slug Shot and tobacco dust are excellent insecticides for aphides and other insect pests; their use, however, leaves the plants in a rather unsightly condition, the leaves being covered with the powder until washed off by rain or the hose, and then again, these insecticides are no more effectual than the clear water applied with force.

A DESTRUCTIVE LEAF MINER

A very destructive leaf miner attacks the leaves of the waterlilies. This has been identified by the United States Bureau of Entomology at Washington, D. C., as the larva of Chironomus modestus, *Say.,* a midge of the family Chironomidae. The larva is very small, from one-eighth to one quarter of an inch in length and about one thirty-second of an inch in diameter. It eats its way along the surface of the leaf, leaving channels behind it that are very unsightly, as well as working considerable damage by weakening the plant through the loss of the leaves. This and all other chewing insects can be kept under control, if not entirely exterminated, by the use of Slug Shot, which is best applied in the dry powdered condition in which it is marketed, by being blown through a powder bellows. It should be applied toward evening, as it will then be more effective, and should be evenly distributed over the surface of the leaves. The leaves can also be sprayed with kerosene emulsion through a very fine nozzle of the Vermorel type, or such as is used for spraying fruit trees with Bordeaux mixture. This will allow of a very fine spray being applied to the surface of the leaves, wetting them thoroughly, with the expenditure of a very small quantity of liquid. For the best results the emulsion should be applied late in the afternoon and every part of the leaves should be coated. These insecticides, if applied as directed, will not harm the fish in the pond. Whatever the material used, it will take several applications to clear the leaves entirely of the miner, which is an enemy that should be watched for closely, and as soon as its work is observed measures should be taken immediately to exterminate the pest.

The Nymphaea Leaf-Beetle (Galerucella Nymphaea, Linn.)

The Nymphaea leaf-beetle is another enemy that causes considerable damage to flower petals and the upper surface of the leaves, especially to those of the Victoria regia. The beetle measures about one-quarter of an inch in length; when matured it lays its eggs on the surface of the leaf in clusters of from six to twenty; they are bright yellow, ovate in form, the larvae are bluish-black above, yellow on the under surface, of elongate form, and when full grown measure three-eighths of an inch in length, widest in the center, tapering toward each extremity. This beetle is very common over the Eastern States, and is reported from many of the Central and Western States, therefore it will soon become general all over the country. Slug Shot, applied in the dry powdered form, will be found a good remedy for this insect. One part Paris green mixed with 50 parts of air-slaked lime or road dust and blown over the leaves with a powder bellows will be found an excellent remedy as well as the above.

An excellent spray for all leaf chewing insects and one that will, if properly applied, soon rid the plants of such, is made by using the following: one teaspoonful Arsenate of Lead paste to one gallon of water, or three teaspoonfuls of powdered Arsenate of Lead to one gallon of water. This to be applied through a spray nozzle that will give a fine misty spray such as the Vermorel.

Other Larval Pests

Another insect that causes considerable damage to the Nymphaea leaves is the larva of the Hydrocampa proprialis. This insect cuts two pieces from the leaves of the lilies and attaches itself between them so that it is completely hidden from sight, as also from its enemies. The pieces of leaves, being lighter than the water, float on the surface, in this way acting as a boat for the insect, which is enabled by this means to be carried by the wind current from one plant to another, eating its way as it goes, very much in the same manner as the bag worm carries its covering around with it when feeding. This is a rather difficult insect to kill. The remedies previously recommended will be effective to a certain extent, but the best method of eradication is to keep a sharp outlook for these small floating pieces of leaves, with the larvae attached, and to crush them. A lamp trap is often suggested to catch the mature insect, but as that instrument never discriminates between friend and foe it is very apt to do as much harm as good. This trap is composed of an ordinary lantern which is stood in a pan of water with a film of kerosene oil on the surface; the insects are attracted to the light and, striking the glass, they fall into the oily water and are killed.

Nelumbiums are often attacked by the larva of Botis nelumbialis. This larva attacks the edge of the leaf, rolling the leaf over itself and gumming it down so as to hold it in position, thus affording the insect a safe place of retreat when attacked. It is a voracious eater and soon destroys entirely the edges of the leaves. The only effectual way to combat this pest is to pinch with the fingers the rolled up edge in which the larva is hidden. This, of course, can only be done in the case of small collections; however, if the work is attended to promptly as soon as the larva makes its appearance, the object can be accomplished quickly and easily. In large collections, where hand extermination is out of the question, the plants can be dusted with Slug Shot or any other arsenical preparation. The kerosene emulsion will not adhere to the leaves of the Nelumbium, therefore is useless against this pest.

A Fungoid Disease

A fungous disease, of the Cercosporae genus, sometimes attacks the leaves of Nymphaeas, causing spots to appear on them and the edges to dry and turn up. This fungus should be checked as soon as noticed or it will spread to other plants. The best results have been obtained by spraying with a weak solution of Bordeaux mixture, using the preparation at about half the strength usually recommended for other plants. This should be applied in the form of a fine, misty spray, thoroughly wetting every part of the leaf. The affected plants should be sprayed every other afternoon until the disease is eradicated. Any of the preparations on the market having sulphate of copper in their composition will check this fungoid growth. It can also be checked by picking off and burning all the spotted leaves. If the leaves are removed and destroyed as soon as the spots are observed, the disease pan be checked or entirely eradicated before much damage is done.

Algae and Confervae

This is a general name given to small fungoid plants that live in the water. They are very destructive to seedling Nymphaeas, adhering to the small leaves and stems and choking the life out of the plants. This fungus is almost sure to make its appearance if a very high temperature has been maintained in the tank, or if too much manure has been used in the soil in which the plants are growing. The growth takes the form of long, green, threadlike stems, closely matted together, and these hold so closely to the plants that it is difficult to remove them. The best remedy is to have plenty of fish in the water and to look closely after the temperature and the manure in the soil.

A very effective means of getting rid of some forms of algae, and especially of that form which is so injurious to the young seedlings, is to use twenty-three grains of copper sulphate to every one thousand gallons of water. This strength will not injure the plants or the fish, but if a greater proportion of copper is employed it is liable to kill both plants and fish.

Rats and Mice

The muskrat is another bad enemy of the water garden. These animals make holes in the banks of the ponds, if of clay. They are partial to the roots of the Nelumbiums, which they soon destroy; they also eat the roots of some of the hardy lilies. Every means should be employed to kill them, such as trapping, shooting, etc. A good way is to set a price on their heads and apprise the small boy that he will get so much for every muskrat he kills. In trapping the muskrat the trap should be set at the opening of the hole, and to one side of it, so that when the rat enters it will be caught by one foot. If the trap is placed in the center of the run there is less chance of catching the animal.

Mice are also destructive, eating both seeds and roots that are stored for spring use; it is well, therefore, to keep the stock where the mice cannot get at it.

In the milder climates, field mice are very destructive to the roots of hardy waterlilies in the winter months, where the water is drawn off and the plants are left in the pond until spring and simply covered with leaves or straw. The best way to get rid of these rodents is by the use of traps that can be baited with grain, or by grain soaked in strychnine strewed in their runs. The latter, of course, should be used with caution and not placed where it may fall into the hands of children or where any valuable animal can get at it.

THE WATER SNAKE

The water snake is another of the enemies of the water garden to be watched for and exterminated. It is very partial to fish and frogs; but as the latter can be dispensed with, if the snake would confine himself to a diet of frogs he would be a benefactor rather than an enemy. It is very exasperating, however, to see a snake in the act of swallowing one of your choice gold fish. These snakes should be killed on sight. It is always well to have a small 22-caliber rifle handy and to be well supplied with shot; for the snake will make its appearance when least expected.

TURTLES

Turtles are also a nuisance and should never be allowed in a pond if it is possible to keep them out, which is not always the case, especially in natural ponds. The turtles destroy the seed vessels of the lilies and the young plant growths.

CRAWFISH

Crawfish are also destructive to the banks of the pond, if formed of clay, which they penetrate, causing leaks at the most unexpected places. An excellent way to get rid of crawfish is to poison some chopped meat with Paris green, placing it around the edge of the pond where they are at work. The meat should be covered, so that while available to the crawfish no animal of value can reach it.

Chapter XXII

GOLD AND OTHER FISH FOR PONDS

IN ponds and other basins or tanks where waterlilies or other aquatic plants are grown, it is necessary to have some kind of fish to keep down insect life in the larval stage, otherwise the ponds will become a nuisance, and countless numbers of mosquitoes be bred and reared to the adult stage in the water. The mosquito must have water in which to deposit its eggs; these are laid in large numbers on the surface of the water. They are long and slender, and stand up side by side. At the end of fifteen days the young larvae hatch and crawl out at the lower end of the eggs; they are then called wrigglers, from the wriggling motion of their propulsion through the water. There are always numbers of them in the rainwater barrel, where they can be studied further. The breathing pore is located near the end of the body; therefore, when at the surface, they always appear head down with this part above the water. The larvae grow rapidly, soon reaching the pupal stage, and in a few days more are transformed into the perfect winged insect. It is in the larval and pupal stages of the insects that the goldfish are most useful as exterminators of the mosquito, as they eat up the wrigglers as fast as they are hatched, never allowing any to reach the winged stage.

This description of the breeding of the mosquito may be thought outside the scope of this chapter, but as every owner of a pond is morally responsible to the general public to see that no mosquitoes are bred in such ponds, too much stress cannot be laid on the fact that, to prevent this, a sufficient number of goldfish should be kept, and one can deal more intelligently with a subject of this character under this full understanding. The fish are also serviceable in keeping in check the black and green aphis. They are also useful in eating up large quantities of the decaying leaves of the water plants.

Only such fish should be used as will not injure the roots or stems of the waterlilies. The best for all purposes is, without a doubt, the goldfish, as they never harm the plants except when young plants have been set out and not properly protected by gravel or coarse sand; in which case they will dig in the soil and very soon have the plants floating on the surface of the water.

The goldfish is very hardy, of beautiful color, and has great variety in form of body, tail and eyes. Especially fine are certain of the fantail goldfish from Japan, some of the rarest of which have been known to command a price of seventy-five dollars per pair. The common goldfish can be obtained in all parts of America at a very reasonable cost. Once a pond is stocked with a few fish, they breed so fast, if afforded suitable protection from their enemies, that where five or six are put into the pond, the year following there will be as many hundreds.

All goldfish belong to the Carp family (Crassius). They are very hardy and easily sent long distances by express.

Goldfish are often attacked by a fungous disease which in appearance resembles cotton wool adhering to the scales or fins. The best treatment for this trouble is to give the sick fish a salt bath, composed of a tablespoonful of salt to a quart of water; in this they should be kept until they begin to show signs of distress by turning over on their sides as if about to die. They should then be put back into fresh water and kept separate from other fish until thoroughly recovered, which will be soon if the disease has not progressed too far. One thing to remember is that in purchasing fish which have been taken from a crowded tank, they never should be associated with other fish until they have been put through this salt bath, otherwise they may bring this fungous growth with them. Similar treatment should be given fish grass, purchased for an aquarium or to be placed in the pond, especially if taken from an aquarium that is overstocked with fish, as the fungus may be transferred with the plants.

The goldfish likes to have a shady spot to resort to when the sun is hot. This shade, in the summer months, will be afforded by the lily leaves and other plant growth. In the aquarium it can be provided by the plants mentioned in the chapter on "Miscellaneous Aquatic Plants."

Goldfish are easily tamed and can be taught to eat from the hand in a little time. If they are fed regularly at the same place they become accustomed to it and will come to that place whenever they see anyone approaching. In the pond it is not necessary to feed the fish as there is always an

The illustrations in the two upper panels show the straight-tailed goldfish. Carassius auratus. (Common goldfish)
This and its many varieties are the best fish for aquaria and waterlily ponds.
The illustration in the lower panel is that of Idus idus (Golden Ide—Golden Orphe) a beautiful yellow colored fish, restless, quick in motion, feeding near the surface, therefore almost always in sight

abundance of insect life there to provide them with food. In the aquarium the fish must be fed regularly, twice a day on suitable food. Do not give them more than they will readily consume at each feeding time, leaving none to decay and pollute the water. An excellent food for goldfish is vermicelli broken up into very fine pieces. Wheat or rice that has been boiled and then crushed is also a suitable food for them.

The goldfish will breed in ponds, tanks, and large aquaria, depositing their spawn among the stems and leaves of submerged plants, to which it adheres; therefore, a number of those plants should always be kept in the water with the fish. The eggs hatch, if the temperature of the water is right, in from four to seven days. When first hatched the fish are very tiny, with a large, round sack attached to the abdomen; this they gradually absorb within a few days. When in the small stage the young fish are dark colored, so that it takes a sharp eye to detect them swimming around just under the surface of the water. This dark coloring is a natural protection to hide them from their enemies. As they get older they go deeper and deeper into the water, until in from sixty to eighty days they begin to take on the beautiful gold color of the adult.

In stocking a pond with goldfish, if one fish for every one thousand gallons of water is allowed, this will be found a good balance. It is not to be understood that no more fish than the number mentioned should be allowed in the pond, but this will be found a good guide in figuring out the number of breeders that should be bought to start with.

The straight tailed goldfish has a plump, symmetrical body, reaching its greatest depth at the beginning of the dorsal and ventral fins. The widest part is at the shoulders, just behind the gill covers near the back; from here the body tapers gradually to the tail. The adult goldfish often reaches a length of from twelve to fifteen inches and a depth of from three to five inches.

The finest and most beautiful of the goldfish family are the Japanese fantailed. They are of bright colors and graceful form, with long, flowing fins and tails. There are five well established varieties of Japanese goldfish that can be bought here. The Wakin (ordinary) is shaped nearly the same as the common goldfish. The body is long and slender, the tail is single or split open, forming a three-lobed tail. This fish is bright gold colored, or variegated with white or black.

The Ryukin, or Loochoo, has a short body and a rounded, bulged abdomen; the tail and fins are long and flowing, often much longer than the body.

The Ranchu, round or lion-headed goldfish, has a rather broad head, a very short, globular body, short tail, and is without the dorsal fin. The old fish develop a number of wartlike protuberances all over the head, making it look like a low coxcomb, hence the name "Lion-head."

The Oranda-Shishigashira, or Dutch lion-headed goldfish, is a cross between the Ryukin and the Ranchu. It has a body somewhat like that of the Ryukin, with the dorsal fin. When two or three years old the wartlike protuberances of the Ranchu begin to develop.

The Deme, or Telescope fish, has large, protruding eyes arranged side-wise on the head. The body is short, of yellowish color, often variegated with black in irregular patches all over the body. In the young state the eyes are about normal, and only begin to protrude as the fish gets older.

"Of all the extraordinary and odd-looking fishes, the Dem-ranchu," says Prof. Mitsukuri, "certainly is far in the lead in many respects, and is interesting as showing how far man can proceed in modifying nature. It is a telescope fish with a short, globular body, without the dorsal fin. The eyes have assumed a most extraordinary position. The ordinary telescope fish is odd enough, with the eyes protruding, but in this variety dislocation has gone one step further.

The eyes have not only started out of the head, but have turned upward 90 degrees, and have their pupils looking straight skyward. For this reason I should be inclined to call this the 'astronomical telescope fish.' As a fish, it is so monstrous that it gives one almost uncomfortable feelings."

ORANDA SHISHIGASHIRA
Lion Headed

The Golden Tench (Tinea aureaus) is another fish suitable for the waterlily pond. It is a handsome specimen, of a beautiful yellow color tinted with deep gold, and spotted with small, irregular black spots. It increases rapidly in the pond, and grows to a length of from ten to fifteen inches. Its habits and food are similar to those of the goldfish.

The Golden Ide—Golden Orphe (Idus idus, Linn.) is a beautiful fish for the pond or aquarium. It is a hardy, graceful, restless fish, always in motion and is therfore more often noticed than the more sluggish goldfish. The back and upper parts of the side are orange colored, with a few black spots, becoming silvery as it nears the lateral line. The fins are white, tinged with silver. This fish grows to a length of twenty-four inches, and is especially desirable for ponds and fountain basins, owing to the fact that it seeks its food in the water near the surface and is therefore nearly always visible, which is not the case with the goldfish. The Ide never burrows in the mud on the bottom of the pond in search of its food; thus the water is kept very clear. The Ide eats small fish, tadpoles and insects; therefore, it is not advisable to have Ides in the same pond with other fish. It increases very slowly, owing to the fact that its spawning time is in April, when there is still danger of enough frost to kill the young.

The Paradise Fish (Macropodus viridus) is a beautiful specimen, well suited for the pond in summer but not in winter as it is very tender and requires to be kept in water above 50 degrees; at spawning time it must have a temperature of 80 to 90 degrees. It is a very lively, voracious fish, eating large numbers of black fly and other harmful insects. The adult fish measures from four to five inches in length. The male is brilliantly colored all over the body; seen in the sunlight his side scales glisten with all the colors of the rainbow. The female is less showy and becomes of a pale whitish color before spawning time. The Paradise Fish should never be placed with other fish or they will immediately attack them.

The fish named above are the best for the water garden for the reasons already stated. It is wise, however, to select one kind, and to have no other fish in the pond, for in changing plants from one pond to another there is always the danger of introducing fish eggs with the plants, thereby getting what may be termed an unwise combination.

Fish that should never be kept with the goldfish are bass, catfish, eels, sunfish, and perch. Frogs and turtles should be debarred as well, as they eat the spawn and the young fish. Another enemy is the water snake, which will consume a large number of the fish.

The little blue heron is a frequent visitor to ponds containing fish, of which it will soon deplete the pond if allowed to. As it is a rather shy creature a man should be secreted in the shrubs or growth around the pond, with a good shotgun, ready to kill the bird on sight. It is frequently claimed that these herons do not catch fish, but merely feed on beetles, etc. This, however, is not the case; they will catch and eat fish as quickly as any other of their foods.

Another robber for which a sharp lookout must be kept is the kingfisher. This bird is well named, for it is indeed a "king of fishers." If a tall tree be near the pond the bird will perch on a branch overhanging the pond whence it swoops down upon the fish, very rarely missing its mark. The kingfisher will also hover on the wing over the pond, circling around it, ready to dart down on a fish at an opportune moment. This bird is a rather small mark for the gunner, but every means should be taken to get rid of it. Sometimes it can be caught in a trap baited with a fish placed where the kingfisher is likely to see it.

Other enemies are the larvae of the dragon fiy, which are very destructive to the young fish as well as to the spawn. The adult dragon flies should be caught with a net and destroyed. Another pest of the fish pond is the water boatman. This insect is about half an inch in length. The body is of a dark brownish yellow. The insect floats on its back, being propelled by two oarlike legs extended at right angles to its body. Its beak is very sharp and capable of inflicting a very severe wound on the hands if the insect is not carefully manipulated. It is especially destructive to young fish. Swimming underneath them, and catching them with its forelegs, it quickly buries its beak in the fish, never releasing its hold until it has extracted all the nutriment it can obtain.

The best way to exterminate all the beetle pests is, wherever it is possible, to have an annual cleaning of the ponds and tanks, drawing off all the water and refilling with clean water. This should be done in spring when the work of dividing and replanting the waterlilies is going on. At the same time the fish can be gone over and the undesirable ones removed. This is necessary to keep the stock pure, as the young of the fantails will sometimes revert to the straight tail, etc.

The following observations on goldfish from an old writer may prove an interesting conclusion to this chapter:

From: "The General History of China," translated from the French of P. Du Halde by R. Brooks, printed in London by John Watts, in 1736:

"The farther Knowledge that I have gain'd from the Chinese who deal in these small fish, and get their livelihood by breeding and selling them, hath given me occasion to make these following observations:

"1—Tho' they are commonly no longer than one's Finger, there are some grow to be as long and as thick as Herrings.

"2—It is not the red or white colour that distinguishes the Male from the Female; the Females are distinguished by little white Spots about their Gills, and little Fins that are near them; and the Males are known by having these Places bright and shining.

"3—Tho' they commonly have the Tail in the shape of a Tuft, yet many have them like those of other Fish.

"4—Besides the small Balls of Paste which they are fed with they give them the Yolk of a boil'd Egg, lean Pork dried in the Sun, and reduced to very fine Powder; they sometimes put Snails into the Vessel where they are kept, because their Slime sticks to the sides of the Vessel, and is an excellent Ragout for these little Creatures, who drive away each other from it that they may suck it themselves; there are also little red Worms found in the Water of some Reservoirs, which they are very greedy of.

"5—It is seldom that they multiply when they are shut up in these Vessels, because their Limits are so small; for if you would have them breed you must put them in Reservoirs, where the Water is fresh and deep in some places.

"6—When the Water is drawn out of the Well to fill the Vessel where the Fish are put, it is necessary to let it settle four or five Hours, otherwise it would be too raw and unwholesome.

"7—If you perceive that the Fish are spawning, which happens about the Beginning of May, you should scatter Grass upon the Surface of the Water that the Spawn may adhere thereto, and when you perceive that the Spawning is over, that is when the Males cease to follow the Females, the Fish must be taken out of the Vessel and put into another, that the Vessel that has the Spawn may be exposed in the Sun for three or four Days, and the Water must be changed in about forty or fifty, because the small Fry begin then to appear distinctly."

Notes

Notes

Notes